# ZHAN

# 站

## Cultivate Your Natural Ability

# MARK STEMPEL

ZHAN

Cultivate Your Natural Ability

print ISBN: 978-1-66787-014-4
ebook ISBN: 978-1-66787-015-1

# CONTENTS

# Dedication

It is with deep gratitude that I dedicate this book to my friend and teacher Fong Ha (1937–2019).

# INTRODUCTION

Growing up in New Jersey, I was always one of the smallest boys in my class. I excelled in mathematics, but, when it came to sports, I did not do so well. I was always the last one chosen for the team. I dreaded going to PE class. I was bullied and picked on for my size. I was often afraid to walk home after school, knowing that I would be stopped and harassed by older boys. I felt weak and was not very confident in my ability to protect myself from abuse. Perhaps it was this experience that inspired me to take up judo and later to study aikido in my early twenties. I wanted to feel strong and safe in a world that often felt scary and threatening.

When I returned to New Jersey after obtaining my M.A. in phenomenological psychology at Duquesne University, a friend of mine introduced me to aikido. I found an aikido dojo about thirty minutes from my home. Besides the philosophy of nonviolence, I loved the flowing, dance-like quality of the art. It was a metaphor for how I wanted to move through my life. I imagined that if I could learn to move with that kind of assurance, I would feel both stronger and safer. After training for two years in New Jersey, I moved to Northern California, where I would continue my aikido training for the next thirty-five years.

Aikido is a Japanese martial art created by Morehei Ueshiba. Ueshiba was a practitioner of Daito-Ryu Aikijitsu who, after a spiritual awakening, left the art to create his own – aikido. Ueshiba, who was under five feet tall, was able to defeat challengers who were significantly larger than he was. He was also able to effortlessly deal with multiple attackers at the same time. He exhibited effortless mastery. He was inspiring to watch. Although Ueshiba himself never taught techniques, his students categorized what he did and created a system of techniques that was passed down. In aikido, we practice set movement patterns. There is an attacker (*uke*) and a defender (*nage*). The teacher will demonstrate being attacked by an *uke* and then defending against a particular attack with a certain technique. All the students will then pair up and practice that attack and that technique. There are tests and ranks as one progresses in the art.

After thirty-seven years of training in aikido, I saw no one who was able to reach the level of mastery that Ueshiba manifested. No matter how hard the students practiced, they were never able to do what Ueshiba did. It was clear to me that just practicing the techniques over and over again would not lead to the kind of transformation I was looking for. In fact, a teacher of mine, Henry Kono Sensei, told me that, when he studied with Ueshiba, he once asked him: "Why can't we do what you do?" Ueshiba's answer was that Kono and others did not understand yin and yang in their own bodies. Like Kono, I wanted to understand yin and yang in my own body.

In my search to understand yin and yang, I met a Chinese *sifu* named Fong Ha. Fong was seventy-seven at the time and had just been diagnosed with stage 4 prostate cancer. He was a small, gentle man with a beautiful smile who reminded me of Yoda from Star Wars. The first time I met Fong, he was unable to cross the street without leaning on me and could no longer teach class. Frankly, it seemed he wasn't going to make it. Three months later, I was shocked when I went to his class in San Anselmo, near where I live in Northern California, to see that he was walking with a cane and teaching *taijiquan*. I could not believe his recovery. I later learned that he had refused all radiation and chemotherapy and had recovered simply through his own *nei-gong* practice. Fong was still quite weak, yet he was able to bounce anyone who touched him. It did not matter where on his body I touched him – his back, his leg, even his head – he was able to move me with no effort on his part. It wasn't his strength – he was seventy-seven and recovering from cancer. It wasn't even technique – he used no set forms that I could see. And although he began studying *taijiquan* with Dong Yingjle when he was fifteen years old, practiced *tui shou* with Yang Sau-Chung, and lived and trained with Han Xing Yuan and Cai Songfang, he claimed that his ability had nothing to do with his training.

I was amazed. I wanted to know how he could move people twice his size with no effort at all. He claimed that this was not some skill he had learned but was a natural ability we all possess. The only difference was that he chose to cultivate this natural ability. The ability he had was like an external immune system. Just as our immune system naturally fights off bacteria, his body seemed to naturally respond to external attacks without direction from his conscious mind. This ability existed in his body. He was not applying some external form. There was no form.

I asked him why, if this was a natural ability as he maintained, he was able to manifest it but I was not. He compared this natural ability to a tree that bears fruit. I was a young tree that had just been planted and was not yet ready to bear fruit. No matter how hard I tried I could not bear fruit because I was not mature enough. Fong seemed to be telling me that this ability to "bounce" people was a natural ability we all have. In fact, when Fong was "doing" something to someone, that was simply his body protecting its own equilibrium. Fong had cultivated this natural ability to maintain balance in all situations. I was looking for Fong to show me how he did what he did, so that I could diligently practice and, after a time, perhaps I would be able to reproduce it. I would quickly learn that this is not how my learning process would unfold. Soon after I met Fong, he told me this story:

> There was once a lion cub who had been orphaned when his mother and father were captured. He ended up living with a flock of sheep and was brought up as a sheep. He came to think of himself as a sheep. When a lion came to attack the flock, he ran away with the other sheep. The lion captured him and asked the young cub why he was running away. The cub said it was because he was a sheep and did not want to be eaten by the lion. The lion grabbed the cub by the scruff of his neck and took him to a small pond and had him look in the water. The lion said: "Look at your reflection. What do you see?" When the cub looked at his reflection, he saw a lion staring back at him. He turned to the lion and asked: "How do I be a lion?" The lion said: "Just open your mouth and roar."

I thought about this story for years. We think we are sheep and therefore we need a shepherd. I felt at the time that I needed someone to show me how to develop the martial skills I was looking to build. I needed a teacher. I wanted Fong to be this teacher. Instead, Fong told me that I was not a sheep and therefore did not need a shepherd. I was just like him, a lion, albeit a young one. He gave me self-awareness. Basically, he told me that I was confused about who I was. I thought I was one thing, but, in fact, I was something else. He could not help me be something I was not. All he could do was to show me my own true nature.

When we look at someone like Ueshiba or Fong we see the fruits of their practice, their ability to neutralize the attack of others and to effortlessly move them. We want to be able to do this ourselves. We focus on what the eyes can see. We focus on the fruit. Show us what to do so we can practice it and also master it. Yet the fruit is simply the manifestation of a process of cultivation. We don't see the cultivation; we only see the fruit. We also fail to ask ourselves why. Why do we want to be able to do this? In my own case it was about fear. Perhaps if I could do this, then people would admire and respect me. My own sense of worth was dependent upon others' recognition of me. This, I was to learn, was simply the hook to keep me cultivating long enough for me to fall in love with the cultivation itself. Rather than cultivating in order to get somewhere, I simply cultivated for the joy of it. Fong would tell a story of slaves on a boat whose legs were chained together so they would all row together. They became very strong and proficient rowers. However, do you think they ever desired to row once they were freed? Cultivation, he told us, is pleasurable; not something that you need to force yourself to do.

What allowed my teacher to perform in the way he did was that his actions were coupled to the world he perceived. I came to understand that the way Fong viewed the world was not the same way I viewed it. I remember one morning at practice there was a dead squirrel next to the tree we practiced around. Squirrels were always running up and down the tree, playing with each other, when we practiced. We dug a hole and buried the squirrel. Burying the squirrel was not an interruption to my practice; it was part of it. Fong's love and care for all life deeply touched me. The world was not a threat and danger to him; rather it was an extension of him. In all the times he bounced me, I never felt he was trying to dominate or harm me in any way. He did not need to make me feel small in order to feel good about himself.

Just as Nisargadatta Maharaj's teacher told him that he was not what he took himself to be, Fong told me that what I am is not what I take myself to be. I am limited only by my own thinking and beliefs. I discovered I was not interested in learning in a conventional way. Instead, I desired to move in my own way – spontaneously, freely and uncontrived. My cultivation process has been about letting go of what all others have told me and discovering my own natural state and ability. I want to share this cultivation process with you so that you too can discover your own original genius. The purpose of this book is not to teach set movements. It is to provide you with a method of accessing your own innate knowing so you are not dependent on me or any external teacher for your learning. It is about supporting you in experiencing your own original genius and expressing that in whatever form you choose. It is my hope that my reflections on my own cultivation process point you to the gate within yourself and inspire you to enter.

# MARTIAL ABILITY

*When you use anything to influence (manipulate and control) others in order to feel safe and valuable, you are avoiding the pain of powerlessness.*

**– Gary Zukav**

## The Desire to Dominate

Much of martial arts is about the desire to dominate and control others and our world. This is the *yi*, the intent. What is missing for many martial artists is any inquiry into their own intent. When we look at our own desire to dominate and control others, we see that it arises out of fear of being dominated and controlled. We live according to a worldview where either I dominate and control you, or you dominate and control me. There are winners and losers. I can get the good end of the stick only if I put you on the shit end. What Ueshiba did was to question this win/lose worldview. The desire to dominate and control means I am out of balance with myself.

Our intent begins to shift. Rather than dominating and controlling others and the world, I seek to know our oneness. I seek to know my source, to know that you and I and all we see come from the same source and are in fact one. We cannot know this oneness if our intent is to dominate and control. Our practice has nothing to do with dominating and controlling anything. Domination and control arise out of duality. Duality arises out of the mind. We are interested in knowing ourselves as we are. We are interested in joining. My sense of self does not depend on making others weak or putting others down. If anything, I am present to awaken all to our true identity. The urge to dominate and control arises out of illusion, out of the belief that you and I are separate and that either I dominate you or you will dominate me. I am calling this choice into question.

My practice has nothing to do with you. I am seeking to know myself, to know the source from which we all arise. The experience of oneness is quite different from the experience of domination. Domination can only exist where there are two. We are interested in transcending this illusion of duality and returning to the experience of oneness. The experience has nothing to do with doing anything to you. When I realize my true identity, I also realize that there is no other. There is only one. It is this experience free of cultural indoctrination that we seek. We seek to see ourselves and the world free of any filter. Direct knowing. Experiencing. A direct experience of our nature as energy. All of these forms, these separations, are created in our minds. They do not exist. A newborn does not experience separation. Separation is learned. Perception is learned. We are taught or brainwashed into seeing the world in a certain way. Yet it is just one way. It reveals not the world as it is, but our structures of perceiving – our beliefs.

So we need to look more closely at our need to dominate and control. We need to allow ourselves to feel the fear of being dominated and controlled. We only agree to mutually beneficial relationships, to engagement for the sake of joining, coming together in celebration, in care, in compassion and understanding. We don't deny our desire to dominate and control and yet we don't act it out either. We examine it. We allow ourselves to feel the fear of being dominated and controlled by others. We can sit with it. Out of this fear of annihilation arises our prayer for healing, for transformation. We allow our hearts to reach out to the spirit of healing, calling in the love and transformation this world so deeply needs.

## Learning and Teaching

What do we learn in the martial arts? How to defend ourselves? From what? Who are we, and what are we defending ourselves from? It's silly to think that it's simply about learning some moves, some techniques, some forms. It's really about the fear we feel and the desire to be safe and to stand up for ourselves. The question is, what do we stand for? It's not about domination and control, although sometimes it is used this way. I want to be stronger than you so I can impose my will on you. I know something, some skill, and I can teach it to you. No. It's different than that.

I am aware of the natural ability each of us possesses as a function of being human. This is the ability to stand and balance on two feet. This is the highest evolution of human beings. We are uniquely able to effortlessly balance on two feet. This is our natural ability. It is unconscious at this point. We don't need to direct the mind to make it happen. In fact, the involvement of the mind interferes with this natural process. So we balance. I balance. It is my nature. It is the nature of the universe to seek balance. Can I allow this process? Balance is alignment with the forces of the universe. It means being in harmony with the force of gravity. No extra effort is required to finding natural alignment. It is not based on how it looks but on how it feels. It is a somatic distinction. We know it in and through our bodies.

Teaching you how to balance is like teaching you how to grow hair. Balancing is your natural ability. We can cultivate it by applying external forces. We do this gradually. I am able to balance when I pick up my coffee cup. My body knows what it needs to do to balance. You don't start trying to walk a tightrope between the towers of the World Trade Center. You work up to it. Nobody said to Philippe Petit, "This is how you do it. You put your foot at this angle and your hand at this position." No. You need to get on the tightrope and do it. You figure it out. This is the blessing my teacher gave me. He said, "Figure it out." I saw what he was able to do and was inspired by it. Yet he couldn't tell me how to do it. He could try but it made little difference. I needed to cultivate my natural ability.

It would be like a young fruit tree asking an older fruit tree how to bear fruit. The old fruit tree can tell the young tree how to do it, but if the young tree is not ready to bear fruit, it makes no difference. Doesn't it make more sense to make sure the young fruit tree has adequate sunshine, water and nutrition so it can fulfill its genetic potential and grow into a beautiful fruit tree? The fruit comes naturally. The martial ability is the fruit. Don't focus on the fruit. Focus on the tree. Care for the tree. Love the tree. The fruit naturally develops. It may be apples, it may be pears – I don't know. It won't be the same as the fruit of the older tree. Yet it will be the fruit of my tree, the manifestation of my natural ability through cultivation. Don't copy the fruit. Cultivate the tree. Experience your tree-ness. Celebrate your tree-ness at whatever stage of manifestation. This is the difference between a copy and the original. I don't want a second-rate copy of your fruit. I want to fully reveal and express the fruit that is mine to share with the world.

## Two Paths

Animals don't practice defending themselves. They naturally do it. It is programmed into their DNA. We don't need to train our immune system to fight off disease. Our immune system will naturally do this. It is designed to fight off disease. Yet if we don't have a strong immune system, it will not do this. We can take pharmaceuticals to fight off the disease, or we can strengthen our immune system. In the same way, we can learn techniques for fighting or we can strengthen our *qi*, our biological life force energy. It is important to see this distinction. When we strengthen our *qi*, we don't just increase our ability to fight off threats. We also improve our health and lay the groundwork for spiritual transformation.

So, the question is, do we want to learn techniques – set movement patterns for dealing with opposition and threats – or do we want to increase our *qi*, our innate capacity to preserve our life? The choice is ours. The important thing is to be clear about what we are doing and why. Are we motivated by fear and therefore want to increase our skills in order to dominate and control, or are we interested in knowing our true nature? Are we interested in knowing ourselves as part of the whole? These are two separate paths. Just be clear which path you are on.

If we choose to increase our *qi*, then how do we do it? We do it by becoming aware of it and no longer depleting it. All of our doing in order to achieve some end depletes our energy. All external movement depletes our *qi*. We need to become aware of it. In order to become aware of our *qi*, we must stop all external movement and come into stillness. In stillness, we turn our attention within. We turn our attention to the bodily felt sense of standing up and not falling down. When we do so, we discover that we balance effortlessly. There is internal movement, constant movement that allows us to stay in balance. Our balance is dynamic and not stable. In other words, our balance is not dependent upon rooting to the ground. We are not a tree. Our balance is dependent upon micro-movements of the autonomous nervous system. We don't cause these micro-movements. They are the system working to maintain equilibrium. When we turn our attention to this process, we discover that the system is working to maintain balance. This is what the system does. This is what every living system does. It seeks to maintain balance.

*Qi* is that which causes us to breathe. It is that which causes us to maintain equilibrium. It is the expression of the intent of the universe to restore balance. If the universe is a living system, then it also seeks to preserve itself and to maintain balance. All movement, all events, are an expression of the universe's desire to maintain balance. This integrative force is what we surrender to and allow to work within ourselves. This movement of *qi* is what brings us back into alignment with nature and with ourselves. The movement cannot be copied. It needs to be contacted from within. We discover the movement within our own bodies. We stop looking for it outside of ourselves. It is the movement of *qi* that sustains us in this very moment. We direct our attention to it and we let go into it. That is the process. We desire to experience it, to feel it working within our own bodies. We do not initiate it. The movement is grace. It is freely given us. We don't need to generate any movement. Our job is to be still, to stop all external movement and enter deeply into stillness. In that stillness, like the black half of the *taiji* symbol, we discover movement, the white dot. We discover movement in stillness.

## Flow of Energy

It's all about intent. Start with why. What is it that I want or that I am after? Mostly it is my own survival. All life seeks to continue to live. This is the operating system. All life seeks to preserve itself. This exists in all life-forms, from cockroaches to lions. They will naturally seek to protect their own lives. They will do whatever it takes. An armadillo will roll up into a ball to protect itself. A possum will play dead. A snake will bite. How about us as human beings? Why do we feel that we need to learn and practice techniques in order to protect ourselves? No other animal needs to do so.

Instead, we are interested in our innate ability to protect ourselves and life. To protect life, we need to first become aware of it. Specifically, we need to become aware of the life force that flows within our own body. Our practice is a practice of awareness. When we stop all doing and turn our attention within, we become aware of what we share with all creation – life. We are alive. There is that which animates us and animates all life. We seek to know this energy within our own bodies, to experience the flow of *qi* within. That is the focus of the practice. In stillness we discover movement. In yin we discover yang, the uncaused movement, the movement of life, the movement of the stars – the expanding universe. We do not cause that movement. It is not mentally generated. It is natural, the movement of life within and without. It is change.

We are simply interested in discovering what is. We are scientists. What is the nature of human beings? What is the nature of life? Life seeks to live. Life seeks to protect and continue its existence. This is the nature of life. We seek to allow the full expression of life within us. We allow life to have its way with us. It's not about going anywhere. It's about seeing where we currently are with new eyes, with the eyes of a child. We look yet we do not see. We are blind to what is actually present, seeing only what is in our own minds. This mentally generated projection does not change the truth of what is present. It only changes what we can see.

So what there is to do is to let go. Relax. Allow. I don't need to do anything. I don't need to change anything. I don't need to repair anything. I simply need to allow. To open and allow *qi* to move. I do this by nonresistance and noninterference. That's all I need to do – nothing. We are not talking about doing. We are talking about cessation of doing – stillness. Not trying to achieve anything. Not trying to make anything happen. Simply letting go. When we let go, we find that life is present. When we let go, we discover that I am. That I exist. We experience this. We experience our own existence. We experience what it is to be alive. We feel it. What is the bodily felt experience of being alive? Of *qi* moving in my body? That is what I am interested in, placing attention on the flow of *qi* within my own body. This is the object of meditation. We experience life as the flow of *qi* within our own bodies. We allow it, we experience it, we welcome it. We cultivate it through awareness.

## Natural Ability

The ability to stand, to balance on two feet, frees our hands to manipulate tools. This standing, this balancing, is the highest evolution of what it means to be human. It is what allows us to use technology. It is from this natural ability that we continue to evolve. We are exploring this ability. If this is what sets us apart, then to understand what it is to be human is to understand what it is to be between heaven and earth, to be balanced between them.

All life seeks to grow. All life will protect itself naturally. This is our right. Do we need to learn techniques to protect ourselves? Do we need to teach our immune system how to fight off bacteria? No. We just strengthen it. It is the same. We don't need to teach ourselves how to defend against outside threats. We simply strengthen our *qi*. How do we do that? We stop using it up. We allow it to build by doing nothing, by simply directing our attention to our *qi* and allowing it to move in whatever way it needs to. We don't need to direct it through our meridians. We allow it to build and to flow throughout our body wherever it needs to go. It's an exercise in awareness of *qi* within you and me. Nothing to do. *Fang Sung*. Release and let go. The process is not directed by our minds. It is opening to the felt sense, allowing the felt sense to direct and move us. It is surrendering to the felt sense. It's not about getting somewhere. It's about coming home to ourselves and knowing ourselves as energy beings. This is not known with the mind. This is felt. In fact, we feel it all the time; we just don't pay attention to it.

There is nothing that I can give you or tell you. I can only reveal you to yourself. I can only point you in the direction. Don't mistake the hand pointing for the moon. Don't seek to be like the masters of old. Seek what they sought. They sought to know themselves and to know the natural ability we have all been given to surrender to something bigger than ourselves. The ability to stand for something. The ability to know ourselves. The ability to live. The ability to love. The ability to move. To open and to allow. The ability to know. These are our natural abilities. Do we need to make ourselves more than what we are? If we know ourselves as all that is, how do we make ourselves more? Let's make ourselves less – less than all we have been told. It is a letting-go process, not an adding-on process. I simply need to let go of the lies I have been told about who I am and why I am here. Releasing all that is not necessary now. I do nothing. I stand. I balance. This is my natural ability. It is yours as well.

# THE INNER TEACHER

*Know that all teachers and techniques are only transitional;*
*true realization comes from the direct merger of one's being*
*with the divine energy of the Tao.*

*- Hua Hu Ching*

## My Teacher's Perception

When I saw how my teacher was capable of effortlessly moving other bodies, I wanted to be able to do that myself. The tendency is to see this as a skill to learn. I can remain the way I am and simply add this skill through learning and practice. Just show me what you are doing, and I will repeat it. Unfortunately, this did not work. Even though he showed me exactly what he was doing, I could not repeat it. Something else was going on. He was not living in the same world I was. In my world, it was not possible to move another human body with no effort whatsoever. In his world, it was perfectly natural. I began to wonder how he perceived the world such that his actions were not only possible, but natural. Action, all action, arises from perception. What occurs is not what causes us to act; our perception of what occurs is what causes us to act. If we want to perform new actions, we must change how we perceive the world.

The way most of us perceive the world is, first of all, that it is separate from us as observers and that all the objects in the world are separate from each other. We assume that this is the way the world is, rather than that we are making this separation. The separation exists in our language. Everything has a name and these names exist in our language. We learn to see a world of separate objects. We are interested in returning to our prelinguistic pre-thought perception of the world. The world my *sifu* saw was one of wholeness. What allowed him to move me so effortlessly was that he was not moving something separate from himself. He was simply moving himself. This perception of oneness allowed him to act the way he did.

My practice became a practice of awareness. The practice is to shift our awareness back to the natural state, perceiving the world as it is. Perceiving the world as it is begins with allowing the world to be just as it is. When we stand in *zhan zhuang*, we are returning to the natural state of oneness. We are already one. We don't need to create or achieve it. It is a fact. All is one. Yet we don't see this because of our habitual ways of seeing, thinking and moving. We have been taught all our lives that we are separate. This is how we see the world. Yet in fact, we are one. So the process is in letting go of everything we have learned about who or what we are. Our identity is tied to habitual ways of thinking, speaking, emoting and moving. It is tied to particular ways of holding our body and to particular tensions in our body. As we *fang sung*, we let go of the partial tension in our bodies. We release our thoughts, our beliefs and our emotions. As we let go, we begin to perceive energy directly. We do this not with our minds, but with our bodies. We turn our attention within to our bodily felt sensations. These sensations exist prior to language. They communicate to us directly. Our intent is to know ourselves and the world as we are – directly – not mediated by language. We seek to know the truth of who we are. This is our *yi*, our intent, and it guides our practice. I am interested in seeing the world as it is, free of all interpretation, perceiving it directly as energy.

## That Which Cannot Be Taken from Us

When I met Fong, he had just discovered he had prostate cancer. He had spent more than fifty years developing his skill, and most of it was taken from him overnight. He was no longer able to balance on one leg. The fact is that the skill we have developed over all of these years will be taken from us as well. Fong grew too sick to even get out of bed, let alone practice *taiji*. It doesn't matter how advanced our skill level is; in the end it is worth nothing. Rather than building something that will be taken from us, something temporal, something limited, we are interested in the eternal. We are interested in that which cannot be taken from us. What cannot be taken from us is who we are. What cannot be taken from us is life, our identity in all that is. What cannot be taken from us is our source, our connection to this source, our identity with this source. What cannot be taken from us is love.

We are interested in cultivating that which cannot be taken from us because it is who we are. We are interested in letting go of everything that is not us, letting go of all beliefs, all understandings, all interpretations of what is and returning to the experience – the direct experience – of what is, prior to all interpretation. We are not learning anything. There is nothing to learn. We are interested in direct experience. We are interested in being. The fact is that we already are. Yet we ignore this. We are so interested in becoming that we forget we already are. We exist. This is what we are interested in becoming aware of, not as a mental idea, but as a bodily felt sensation. We explore this. We return to this. Not being a man, or being old, or being a martial artist. None of this. We are simply interested in the being-ness, the is-ness. We are interested in what allows this. What is the source of being? The source of life? The source of all that is? Whatever it is, it is the same for all of us. We all come from the same place and will return to the same place. This is our equality.

The process is a process of letting go and surrendering into who we are. We don't need to do it. We don't need to make it happen. This is what we become aware of. There is movement, but we are not doing it. We are not making the movement happen. We can choose to be aware of our participation in the movement of life. Life is energy and energy moves. We allow this. We are creating the space, through our relaxation, for the free movement of *qi*. The movement removes all obstacles. Life is a river flowing: as the quantity of water increases, it removes all blocks in its way. Cultivating our *qi* is the increase in the quantity of water that flows. We focus on this. We are unconcerned about the obstacles. We focus our awareness on our own *qi*, our own capacity to balance through movement.

This experience of oneness cannot be taken from us because it is the truth. It is what is so. We are a part of all that is. This experience of oneness is what we all seek, whether we know it or not. No material thing can give us this experience because it is what we already are. It is when we turn our attention from the material world to our inner experience that we realize who we are is one with all that is. Death is simply the final letting go. It is part of a process of letting go that we are engaged in. Death is simply a part of this letting-go process. The practice is one of relaxation and release. This process continues.

## Open Your Mouth and Roar

What is a teacher? We are all teachers. The question is, what do we teach? Do we teach separation or unity? Do I think that I have the answers – that I know and you do not? That only through me will you find the way? This is a lie. Each of us, everyone, is part of God and one with God. We may not have that awareness. We may not be awake to the fact that we are one with all that is. As a teacher, I can only help you remove the blocks to the awareness of your true identity. I cannot give you anything. I can only take from you what is not yours – the lies and deception, the false beliefs, the misunderstandings. When I take these away from you – invite you to let them go – your true identity is revealed. I cannot, nor do I desire to, tell anyone how to move or how to breathe. I want to support people in finding and connecting with their own inner knowing. When I was originally looking for a teacher, I thought I was a sheep looking for a shepherd. My teacher, a lion, took me by the scruff of my neck and brought me to the water. He had me look at my reflection in the water. Lo and behold, I saw another lion. I asked him, "How do I be a lion?" He told me I already am a lion, to just open my mouth and roar. That is what I am doing now. I am a lion, not a sheep. I do not need a shepherd. I only need to open my mouth and roar.

The teaching is inside of me. I am the teaching. My nature is the teaching. My work is to uncover it. To relax, release and let go of everything that is not me, all of the lies, the social conventions and agreed-upon understandings of what the hell is going on around here. I was born into this world, into these bands of awareness. This is a world we have made. It is not the real world. The real world is eternal. The real world is what God created, not what man has made. This is an important distinction. We fail to differentiate between dream and reality, between what God created and what man made.

It is time for me to stop looking outside of myself for answers, to stop looking for someone who knows, who can tell me, who can awaken me. How did Osho awaken? Ramana Maharshi? Nisaragatta? It was their desire. It was how much they wanted it. It was everything to them, the most important thing. They dedicated their life to waking up. This is what matters. The strength of your desire for union and oneness, for truth. Let go of the need to dominate and control. Let go of the need to be top dog. Let go of all of it to discover what is left, who or what I am. It is this desire or longing for union that can guide and teach us.

I don't need acknowledgment from others to know I am on the right track. It is not about getting anywhere except right here and now in this moment. There is nothing to achieve, nothing to attain. It has already been achieved and attained. The great accomplishment is who I am. Life. The infinite expression of *qi*. This is God. This is who I am at my core – this *qi*. I share this with all of creation. I am not separate. I am one with all that is. I discover my oneness. My self is revealed when I let go of all that is not me. This is the letting-go process.

## Internal Knowing

I will not turn over my authority, my knowing, to others. This is what the culture says: "You know nothing. We will teach you all you need to know." We depend so much on authorities. We can't even give birth (the most natural process) without experts. This reliance on experts disconnects us from our own knowing and intuition. A good teacher does not develop a dependency with his student. It's not like I have all the answers and if you study with me, I will give them to you. The artist who walked the tightrope between the towers of the World Trade

Centers wasn't shown a technique. No, it required a refined, somatic distinction of balance.

This somatic exploration is not something someone can do for you. You have the opportunity to explore it yourself. This is not about technique or doing it right. It has nothing to do with dominating others. It has to do with turning the attention within. What is my experience of standing? What is my experience of balancing? What does it feel like? Can I recognize when I am balanced and when I am off balance? The system will naturally return to balance. The system seeks balance. This is *Taiji*. The Great Ultimate. From nothing a point. One creates two. Two creates many. We trace it backward. From many we go to two – all things are either in movement or stillness. From two to one. Movement and stillness are the ultimate poles of one process, *Taiji*. In movement we discover stillness and in stillness we discover movement. Stillness is movement slowed way down. One. In this oneness we discover emptiness – nothingness – a return to the source. These are just words. What matters is the felt sense. This is what we are inquiring into for the sake of truth, for the sake of joining with all that is.

We all want the fruit. A good teacher shows us how to plant the seed. The seed is *yi*. The seed is our intent. Do we want to dominate and control, or do we want to join? Our desire to dominate and control arises out of our sense of separation. Yet this sense of separation is itself an illusion. We are not separate. Without our environment – air, water, people – we would not exist. So who or what are we attempting to dominate and control? Fear is a lack of the awareness of love. Turn the light on. The light is our awareness, our *shen*. Pay attention to what is happening inside. There is nothing to achieve. You are already it. You are. I am. I exist. That is enough. That is a miracle. Life is a miracle. Presence. Life flows in and through me, just as it flows in and through you. The same *qi* flowing through all. One energy. The energy of life – the springing forth, the expression of itself. What is there to learn? The process is one of unlearning who we have been told we are and discovering what is so.

## The Purpose of a Teacher

We are constantly looking outside of ourselves for answers. I discovered that, even if my teacher had the answer and could tell me, it didn't make a difference. I still could not do what he could do. It is not just a question of knowing with our minds and then instructing our body to do it. Our bodies are not capable of doing it. It requires that we cultivate something in our bodies. What we are cultivating is an awareness of balance, not a mental awareness of balance, but a bodily felt sense of balance. This is what my teacher had. He embodied a refined sense of balance. It is this distinction – this somatic distinction of balance – that opened up new possibilities of movement for him. Copying his movements is not the same as cultivating the somatic distinction of balance. Just doing the movements doesn't lead to a refined sense of balance. That is working from the outside in. In internal arts, we work from the inside out. We shift the way the world shows up for us by further embodying distinctions in our body. We cultivate this through non-doing and awareness.

A teacher serves to show us what is possible, to point us in a direction, to open the door. Yet we are the ones who need to walk through. A good teacher, a true teacher, can only open our eyes and awaken us to who we are. What he can do is to take away what we do not need, our illusions about who we are. He cannot give us anything. He can only share his self with us. In that process we recognize that this is our self too, that we are one with each other and all that is.

This is an awareness. The actions that arise out of this awareness are different than the actions that arise out of illusion. We are interested in seeing. We are interested in seeing energy. When we remove all of the obstacles to seeing things as they are, we recognize that we are one with all that is. We have no form. We are no thing. We seek not a mental awareness, but a bodily felt sense of our own nature. This is why we stand – to know ourselves directly, to know our nature. All arises out of and returns to this.

It's not a question of practicing certain movements. The question is: "From where does the movement arise?" Is it mentally generated movement, or is it movement that precedes the mind? Movement that is not directed by the mind? True movement? We discover this in stillness.

# ZHAN ZHUANG

*If we surrendered*
*to earth's intelligence*
*we could rise up rooted, like trees.*

*- Rilke*

## Mother Earth

The essence of our practice is to bring awareness to our relationship with the earth, beginning with our actual physical relationship to it. We call this gravity. It is the attraction of our physical bodies to the earth. We can feel this when we stand. We drop everything. We allow everything to return to the earth. We practice dying. It is this letting go, this dropping it, that is the doorway to our art. We give. We give it all to the open arms of Mother Earth. And she receives it willingly, thankfully. When we let it go, we experience emptiness, openness, space. And into this space she fills us with source energy. We allow the life-giving energy of the earth to rise up in us. We are available to this energy because we are no longer holding and bracing against the earth.

Mother Earth shares her abundant love with us. There is a rising up, a reaching for the stars. This is the energy that has allowed us to stand up, to build skyscrapers, to create rocket ships. This is our use of *qi*. Yet *qi* has its own purpose of enlightening, of waking us up to our true identity as the opening for this force to emerge. In other words, all of our problems and concerns come back to this primary relationship with Mother Earth. We have many feelings about being here that we are unconsciously acting out in our culture. We seek to dominate her, to use her, to take from her. But do we know her? Do we hear her? Do we feel her? Do we appreciate her? If not for Mother Earth we would not exist. Without the earth we cannot survive. She gives freely and generously to all. She also receives. She receives our hurt, our fear and our frustrations. She also receives our gratitude.

Truly our practice is all about our connecting link with Mother Earth. We are cleansing this link, removing the blockages, allowing *qi* to flow more freely through our system. The energy itself cleanses. We simply need to bring our awareness to it. As we appreciate it, it grows. It's not about doing anything. It's not about changing anything. It is simply about where we place our awareness. Whatever we focus on grows. What do we choose to be aware of? I am inviting you to be aware of your body's relationship with the earth: not a mental awareness, a bodily felt sense of your relationship with Mother Earth. This is the doorway.

## The Energy of Return

We have severed our connection with nature. Basically, we have said that nature is an inanimate object separate from us. We then go on to manipulate and control her. But nature cannot be controlled. Nature is the manifestation of God/Goddess in this world. Nature includes our human bodies. All form, all manifestation, is an expression of the unmanifest – of God. Our relationship with nature is not one of control. It is one of nonresistance. Nature is the will of God. We are one with nature. We share the same source. Wherever nature came from, we also came from that place. The process is one of return. It is one of letting go of all we have built up to protect us from the natural world. We once again return to our primary relationship with the earth. We actually feel her underneath our feet and we surrender our mass to her. We allow ourselves to be supported by Mother Earth. She is nourishing us, providing for us. We simply acknowledge it and allow gratitude for Mother Earth to be present in our hearts.

All illness, all disease, is a function of our losing awareness of our connection, our oneness, with Mother Earth. We seek to return to this awareness of oneness. We do this physically by turning our attention to our actual physical connection to Mother Earth. We become aware of our feet touching the ground. We are physically connected to Mother Earth. She provides all of our sustenance. We forget. We are not independent of the earth. Gaia is one system, one being. We are a part of the Gaian system. We let go of who we think we are and return to the bodily felt sensation of standing on the earth. She receives everything. She receives our anxiety, our fear, our sadness, our anger. She holds all of it in a loving embrace.

One way or another, everything returns. We can attempt to block this return, but in the end it triumphs. We let go to this. If we do not return of our own free will, then we will return eventually anyway. All things return to the earth from whence they were born. We were born of our Mother and return to our Mother. Choose to return or return anyway. Return of your own free will or return kicking and screaming, but return you will. We bring our awareness to the returning energy. We call this gravity. It is the attraction of our bodies to Mother Earth. It is the pull between our body and the earth. We allow this. We bring our awareness to this pull and in doing so we recognize our oneness. We don't need to make it happen. It is happening. Our body is magnetized to Mother Earth. We are connected, made of the same substance. Our body is the earth. There is nothing to do. There is a process that is already happening. It is a physical, emotional and spiritual process. It is the movement toward oneness. We find this movement in stillness. In stillness, life force congeals. It comes together and rests in the loving arms of Mother Earth.

## Health

What is health? Health is the free flow of *qi*. When *qi* is stagnant, then there is disintegration, rotting and so forth. We need to allow the free flow of *qi* in and through the system. It does this naturally. It finds its way, like water. Like water flowing, we can remove the obstacles. We can purify the system. Or, better said, when *qi* flows freely, the system is purified. It is like allowing pure water to run through our pipes. It flushes everything out. We can also use herbs and elixirs to weaken the hold of parasites and toxins in the system so they can be removed more easily. We are interested in the natural functioning of the system prior to the introduction of toxins. When our *qi* is strong, we are protected from the intrusion of outside energies. Our job is to strengthen *qi* through inner cultivation. Energy follows awareness. By placing our awareness on *qi*, we allow it to grow, to strengthen.

Health is our natural state. We were created healthy. We need to stop doing those things that take us out of a healthy state. The most important is toxicity, the blocks to the free flow of *qi*. As we cultivate *qi*, the blocks are of no concern. They cannot withstand *qi*. There is that which is dying and that which is being born. We need to allow this process. Allow what needs to die to die. We hold on and try to protect it, try to keep it alive, but it needs to die. Allow the disintegration, the dying, so something new can come forth. We are interested in returning to our natural state of oneness. This is the state of *wuji*, no separation, not two. This is the state from which we arose and the state to which we will return. We release all that does not belong to the earth. The earth gladly receives it.

The Aztecs worshipped a goddess named Tlazolteotl. She was the goddess of both shit and love. I was confused by this. How could she be the goddess of both shit and love? I realized she was able to receive everything in love. Everything. All of my shit, my hatred, my fear, my desire for revenge, my blaming, my anger. All of it. With an open heart. She could take it all in, knowing it is not my essence. She desires to receive it. It is the Goddess, Mother Earth, that I am releasing it all to. And she receives it all in love. She grounds it, takes it into her molten core and allows it to burn. In fact, it is food to her. It feeds the fire of her love. When you stand on the earth, feel the love of Mother Earth, her willingness to support you and to receive all that you offer. It may be shit to you, but it is food to her. It is out of this fecundity that something new is born. Something new is sourced. The process is *fang sung*. It is letting go and releasing into receiving arms. Letting go, we feel the love and support. We feel fully received. We don't need to hide the darkness. We don't need to hide any of our feelings. She lovingly receives it all, and it makes her stronger. She eats it. All of it. She receives our poison and it is transformed. It is food, natural fertilizer. Love overcomes all. It receives all.

## Self-Regulation

You don't need to receive any special knowledge or skill. That's really what it comes down to. We are exploring the nature of being human. We are exploring the nature of standing up and not falling down. We are exploring what is so, what is true about ourselves. We don't need to change ourselves, to improve ourselves or to learn new knowledge or skills. We are simply exploring what it is to be in a body, to stand up and not fall down. We are exploring verticality. What is the nature of standing up and not falling down? What is the nature of balancing? What is the nature of using minimal effort? These are the vital questions we are exploring. What is the nature of our relationship with heaven and earth? Not words. The answer to this question is what we are currently experiencing. What is the felt sense of standing up and not falling down? What is the felt sense of using minimal effort? These are the questions that this practice explores.

What does it take to stand up and not fall down? When I slip on a banana peel, I don't need to tell my body how to regain balance. The system is designed to maintain equilibrium. Earth and all of its inhabitants are part of a self-regulating system always seeking balance. This system is working within me as well. It sustains me. I don't need to tell my lungs to breathe and my blood to flow. I don't need to direct it with my conscious mind. I don't need to make the earth go around the sun either.

It is not moving from outside; it is moving from inside. *Qi* moves and I allow it to move me. First I have to feel it, feel my mass. I must have awareness of my mass in relationship to the earth. There is an attraction. We call it gravity or magnetism. My center is connected to the center of the earth easily and naturally. I don't need to make it so. I am not aware of it because of the partial tension in my body. The first step in standing is to let this go. Well, perhaps the first step is to become aware of the tension, the places in my musculature that I am holding. We can begin to let this go through standing and through loving touch. It is not required in order to stand. Release unnecessary tension. Or release unnecessary contraction. Tension-Charge-Discharge-Relax. Through loving touch we can release the unnecessary tension. Release yourself into the middle of the stream instead of hanging onto the banks. Just let go. Letting go is not doing. We simply cease holding on. We stop doing. Our doing is no longer necessary. It is a doing that we are not conscious of. We bring that doing to consciousness. Perhaps it is bracing. We are only trying to protect ourselves from being hurt. However, it is not necessary. Life, which we are, cannot hurt us. It is not against us. It is not separate from us.

## Zhan Zhang and Shi Li

As a teacher, I can only reveal to you what you already are, the miracle that you are. I cannot add one cubit to your height. It is not about learning new skills or accumulating more knowledge. It is about knowing ourselves as we are. You are the same as me. The life energy that flows through me flows through you. We are no different. What is possible for me is also possible for you. It is not – I know – I am special – I am enlightened. If you spend time with me, if you study with me, than you too can learn what I know, but you must listen to me. You must give up your individual will and surrender to me. This is not it.

Aikido is the way of harmony with *qi*. The fact is that we are already in harmony with *qi*. We are in harmony with the force of gravity, but we are not aware of it. We take it for granted. In standing meditation we redirect our awareness to standing up and not falling down – our balance or equilibrium. We feel directly what it is to be in harmony with gravity. There is a bodily felt sense to this that we have blocked from our awareness. We return to this bodily felt sense and we pay attention. By paying attention to it, we cultivate harmony with gravity. We then expand on this experience. We cultivate this experience while moving our bodies. The standing we call *zhan zhuang* and the moving we call *shi li*. *Zhan Zhuang* and *shi li* are in fact one because movement and stillness are one. Without movement there is no stillness and without stillness there is no movement.

So, again, we are not learning new skills we can use if we are attacked. We are cultivating the experience of being in harmony. We are bringing this to awareness, and we are protecting this experience of standing up and not falling down. This seems pretty clear. We are doing it for the sake of harmony with *qi*. In other words, we are doing it for our own well-being and for the well-being of others and the earth.

True movement arises from stillness, not from others telling me how to move. What we are engaged in is no method, no teaching. There is nothing to do and nowhere to go. There is only here and now. We stop doing, stop achieving, and simply experience what is. We experience standing up, not falling down. Balancing. How does that live in your body? What is the bodily felt sense of standing up and not falling down? That is our inquiry. It is a training of awareness.

Again, when we engage with others, we are simply paying attention to standing up, not falling down. Our bodies will do whatever they need to do to not fall down. I don't need to give you techniques for not falling down. When your body slips on a banana peel, it knows exactly how to regain balance. The same is true if someone attacks you. Your body will protect your equilibrium – this is what it is designed to do. We simply need to let the system work. We need to get out of the way with our minds and let the body do its job.

Learning techniques for regaining balance is not necessary. We are in a canoe on a river that is flowing downstream in the direction we want to go. We don't need to spend our time learning new paddling techniques. We can relax, lean back and enjoy the ride. The river is taking us where we want to go. Enjoy the scenery!

# FANG SUNG

---

*Sung can be translated as: the systematic transference of habitual tension from either the physical or consciousness body into the energetic realm.*

**– Damo Mitchell**

## Fang Sung

It starts with *fang sung*: letting go, releasing, letting the weight drop, allowing the skeleton to hold you up. All weight (mental, emotional, physical) drops to the earth. Feel the connection with the earth. There is a natural downward force – some call it gravity. Let yourself feel that natural force in your body. Let everything go. You still stand. You still reach for the sky. So there is another force, the force of life, the force of growth. To experience that force, we must let go. Drop it. Sometimes we are in conversations in which we know there is no resolution. We just drop it. We let go. As long as the monkey holds onto the fruit, he cannot remove his hand from the cage. We need to let go of the fruit if we want to be free. What is the fruit? It is what we are holding on to – power, domination, riches. It is the struggling and trying to achieve. We drop it – this is *fang sung*. We drop it and we discover we are supported by the earth in many ways. The earth provides us with a ground to stand on. It provides us with air to breathe, water to drink and food to eat. Mother Earth truly sustains us. As long as we are holding on, bracing, trying to sustain ourselves, we cannot experience the sustenance of Mother Earth. What she says is that I can hold all of your burdens; let them go. Once we do, we experience the strength of Mother Earth rising upward in our bones, Mother Earth responding to the warmth of the sun, opening to love.

The first step is *fang sung*. Am I willing to let go? When I let go, I discover I am connected to the earth. I am supported and sustained by the earth physically. My body has a relationship to the earth. They are made out of the same stuff. When my time here is over, my body will return to the earth. When we let go, there is space. Something comes to fill that space. That is life force – energy – *qi*. We create the space for *qi* to flow. *Qi* is already present inside and outside. When we release the contraction – the holding – we create space in which *qi* can flow freely. Try it now. Stand. Just stand. Allow your weight to drop. Allow everything to drop. Pay attention to the feeling. This is the essential part. It's not what you do that matters – it is experiencing it. Be present to the sensation of letting go. What does it feel like in your body? What do you notice? There are no wrong answers here. Your experience is valid. We stand a lot. Waiters stand. Guards stand. But do they pay attention to the internal sensations of standing? What is their *yi*, their intent, in standing? Our intent is to be present, to be aware and to fully experience standing. What allows us to stand, to be balanced? It is not our thinking minds. Something else is at work here. We are in harmony with all that is. We don't fall down. This is *Taiji*. This is harmony. We don't do it. We are already in harmony, in balance. We simply stop trying and experience what it is to be in harmony.

## Gnosis

Our practice is not a doing. It is a non-doing. In practice we drop everything. We release and let go. We *fang sung*. We drop it. Everything else in our lives may be about doing, about accomplishing, achieving, producing some result. In practice we stop. And in that stopping, we simply are. We allow ourselves to rest in being, to rest in the earth, to be supported by the earth. We stop searching and are simply present. We are present with our bodies and the bodily felt sense of standing up and not falling down. We are not doing it. We are not consciously making ourselves balance. We discover something else is at work here, and we are not doing it. Our balancing is like the earth circling the sun. We don't need to make it happen. There is an intelligence that is not the conscious mind, a deeper knowing. It is this deeper knowing that we surrender to, an innate intelligence in our bodies. This innate intelligence has us vomit when we have eaten something toxic. It is a knowing in our bodies, a knowing prior to words. We have lost touch with this. Now women cannot do the most natural act of giving birth without consulting an expert. We have been taught not to trust ourselves, not to trust each other, not to trust our bodies. Trust only the authorities. We know nothing. We can't even take care of ourselves without the system, without the experts.

*Gnosis* means inner knowing. We stop looking for a teacher to give it to us. We stop looking outside and turn our attention inward. We open to the innate wisdom of human being with millions of years of experience. That experience, that human wisdom, lives in our own DNA. We open to this. We open to the wisdom contained in our own bodies. Our bodies are not a blank slate. We are not monkeys to be trained to perform certain movements. There is that which is inside of us. There is the spark of life. *Qi* has given birth to us. We are an expression of that *qi* and we open to it; we allow it. This *qi* is who we are. It is what animates us. We seek to allow this energy to move. We need to create a space for it. We need to stop adding things and return to what is. We stand up and don't fall down. We are not consciously doing it. This is grace given to us. We are supported by the earth and we open to and acknowledge this support.

We are not trying to get anywhere or to attain anything. We are simply seeking to know ourselves as embodied human beings, as part of something much bigger than we are, something that has its own purpose. Life has its own purpose in which we are all included. We all have a part to play in the larger purpose of life, here and now. We don't need to figure it out. We are already serving the purpose for which we were created. We seek to know this. Or rather, to have an experience of the purpose, the intelligence of *qi*. Life is not a mistake.

So we open. We let go of all we think we need to do, all we have been told we need to do. There is nothing to do. It has all been done. All has been accomplished. Life is the great accomplishment, not the accomplishment of men, but the accomplishment of God/Goddess/All That Is. That accomplishment is you and me and all we see. That great accomplishment is the life of which we are a part.

## Multidimensional *Fang Sung*

*Fang sung* is the doorway. It is about releasing and letting go, no longer holding on to anything. Really, in the end, we will need to let go. We don't wait until the end. We let go now of all that no longer serves us. We just drop it, not holding on to our idea of what is happening here, not holding on to grievances. We just drop it. We let it go and feel a little more space in our hearts. We let go of grievances against those who have harmed us in some way. *Fang sung* is not just releasing muscular tension – it is releasing everything that is not needed in order to stand here. We drop all tensions, armoring, grievances, emotions, ideas, perceptions and habits that do not serve us. We no longer hold the past against ourselves or others. What happened, happened.

We release the gall, anger and resentment from our livers: the anger about what happened, the resentment toward those who hurt us. Just let it all go. In the end, we will need to let it all go anyway. Yes, it starts with a physical letting go of unnecessary holding in the body, but it does not stop there. It is letting go of all of the holding, everywhere we are holding on to something. We simply open our hand and drop it. We did not know we were holding. This is what *Zhan Zhuang* shows us. It shows us all of the places where we are holding on, where we did not realize we were expending energy to hold on. We just stop doing it. It is as if our hands are in fists and we were not aware of it. We just let go. We let our hands relax. This is *fang sung*. This is the doorway into internal energy arts. We stop trying to control everything and allow things to be just as they are.

It's like a dog who has our shoe in his mouth. We say, "Drop it." Just drop it. What is the shoe in your mouth? What is it you are holding on to and won't let go of? Here is your opportunity to drop it. It is about cleansing, releasing, letting go. This is the process. It is not a process of addition. It is a process of subtraction. We release all that we don't need, all that is not ours, and in doing so we discover what is essential. We discover who we are. We are not trying to achieve or attain anything. We are simply letting go. I don't need to hold this anymore. I don't need to carry this backpack of bricks anymore. I don't even know why I thought I needed to. I am aware that it is heavy and not comfortable and I don't need it. I am just going to let it go. I don't need to carry it anymore. This is *fang sung*. This is a process. So this is what we do. We release it all. We let it drop into the earth. We don't need to carry it anymore. When the end comes, there is nothing to let go of. We have already let go of everything that is not who we are, everything that is not essential to live. It's a spring cleaning.

## The Preexisting Program

In *zhan zhuang* we discover our equilibrium. In *shi li* we experiment with it. We allow our equilibrium to move. The equilibrium naturally moves. The movement happens to maintain equilibrium. This is our natural ability. We experience this as the movement of our equilibrium. The movement of our center of balance. We allow this movement. We join with this movement. It is the movement from yin to yang and back to yin. The movement from *wuji* to *taiji*, from undifferentiated oneness – *wuji* – to the two ultimate poles – *taiji*.

The movement itself is healing. This movement – this natural balancing process – is a healing movement that brings *qi* to all parts of the body. Naguchi calls it Katsugen – the regenerative movement. The movement is balancing. The movement itself is brought about by the stabilizing muscles, those muscles not controlled by the conscious mind. The intent of this movement is to be in harmony with gravity. When we surrender and allow this movement, it brings us into balance with the earth and sky. The intent or purpose of the movement is to restore balance, the physical expression of the Holy Spirit and of God's will. Oneness, harmony, balance. The movement itself seeks to restore balance to the system. This movement exists within you and me. It is our gift, our inheritance, our natural ability as human beings.

Only in the state of *sung* can we discover this movement. We need to release control of the conscious mind. We need to stop running all our software programs. We need to wipe the disk clean to discover the operating system that already exists, the preexisting program called life. This is not a man-made program. It is the program we came in with, the one that makes the earth orbit around the sun, the one that makes night and day and brings the rain. That one.

## Surrender Now

Yielding to the force of gravity doesn't mean ending up as a pile of flesh on the ground. We yield all unnecessary effort – all muscular tension that is not required to stand. We depend on the bones to support us, not the muscles. We don't need to create a structure, muscles, because we have a preexisting structure, bones. It really is essentialism. What is essential here? We focus on the 80 percent of the results that come from 20 percent of the effort. We just need to clarify what that 20 percent is. It is not technique. It is not about taking direction from outside of myself. It is about looking within, accessing my own inner knowing and not looking outside of myself for someone to show me or teach me. It is clarifying my intent: is it to dominate or to share? There is more than enough for all of us. I don't need to put others down so I can feel good about myself. I am equal to all that is, no better and no worse. We are one. What benefits me benefits you. We are all seeking connection. Yet we find that connection inside of ourselves, the connection to qi. I don't need to improve myself. I don't need to make myself worthy in the eyes of God. I simply love myself as I am now.

The process is one of letting go, of cleansing the doors of perception so we can see what is actually present. The world we see is colored by the lens we look through. We are interested in cleansing the lens. The lens is everything we have been taught about the world. Actions arise from our perception of the world. If we want to change and transform the world, we must change and transform the world we see. It is colored by past traumatic experience, by cultural beliefs and prejudices. We do not know the world, nor do we know ourselves.

What we see with our eyes is the world man has made and believes is real. It is a figment of his imagination. What is the world you dream of? What is the world you want to see? It exists; we are just looking in the wrong place. It is not out there. It is inside. That is the domain we practice in. We are interested in the world inside, the world each of us has our own access to. We stop the external world. We stop the doing, the grasping, the trying to achieve. We allow the external world to be just as it is and we turn our attention within. This is crucial. We are interested in what is here, what is actually present, in feelings, sensations, thoughts, intuitions, bodily felt sensations prior to any interpretation, raw data.

It is out of our dissatisfaction with the external world that we let go of and turn within. The external world is a reflection of what is in all of our hearts. The work of purification is done within. We are cleansing the internal domain. We are letting go of all that we no longer need. We are just letting go now, releasing. And in that releasing we are creating space, lots of space. That is what we are left with when we *fang sung*. Lots and lots of space.

# BALANCE

*Human upright standing, loosely referred to as posture, is
not governed by the laws of static equilibrium.*

*- Moshe Feldenkrais*

## Not Learning Movements

It's not about learning a specific technique or movement. In the end,
no technique or movement will keep death away. I am not learning
techniques or movements; I am learning to yield. I am learning to let
go, to surrender to *qi*. That is my practice because, in the end, that is
what I will need to do. I will need to let go. Why not learn to do that
now? Why not learn to let go now? In fact, I don't need to learn to do
it. It is not a do. It is a cessation of doing. It is recognizing that there
really is nothing to do. It is already done. Can I acknowledge it?

So please don't teach me movements. Don't teach me how I
ought to do it. The "right" way is different for each one. It arises from
within. What do I need to do to maintain balance when I slip on a
banana peel or when I cross a tightrope? What matters is the feeling,
the felt sense of being in balance. This is the guide to maintaining or
allowing this felt sense. Do I know what it feels like to be in equilibrium? Yes, I am in equilibrium. But do I pay attention to it? It is an

exercise in awareness. Where is my awareness? What is it I am paying attention to? That is the question. What am I paying attention to?

I don't want to learn a set of movements. I want to allow my movement to arise out of stillness, to naturally arise from within. I want movement for movement's sake, not to defend myself. What do I need to defend myself from? Am I separate? If I am one with all that is, why do I need to learn to defend myself? There is no threat. There is only love. This is the truth. If I don't see it, then there is something wrong with my seeing. I am seeing that which is not there.

Let me see things as they are. When I do, I see we are all one. We are all *qi*. I can intend to be in harmony with *qi* or try to manipulate it and control it. What does it mean to be in harmony with *qi*? It means allowing it. It means relaxing, releasing and allowing the flow of *qi*. That is really what it comes down to: relaxing, releasing and allowing all of it, just as it is, to be. That is the practice – relaxing, releasing and allowing.

## Balancing Is a Natural Ability

*Yiquan* is not about learning new skills, techniques or movement patterns. We are not trying to change you, improve you, make you better. You were created perfect. Yiquan starts with a feeling and with a desire to know yourself. It begins with a desire for wholeness, for oneness, for love, for light, a desire to know one's true nature. It begins in stillness. We turn our attention from the outside world. We stop all doing, all achieving, all struggle, and simply be. We stand on two feet. This is what makes human beings unique. We ask the question: "Who or what am I?" The answer we are looking for is not a mental construct. It is a bodily felt sensation. We look to our feeling bodies to provide an answer. What we find when we are standing still is that we balance. We do not fall down. We don't need to use our minds to balance. We balance naturally. In effect, there is a program functioning – no, not a program. It is part of the operating system of human beings. My body stands up and does not fall down through no conscious effort of my own. This in effect is a miracle. If I slip on ice, my body will naturally attempt to restore balance. It is this natural ability that we seek to know, to become intimate with, to cultivate. We do this through our awareness. We turn our awareness to the natural ability of balancing. We discover the body is always balancing. In order to balance, it needs to change. The body is alive and constantly changing in order to maintain its equilibrium. We track these changes in our body with our awareness. We allow them.

We are not learning new skills in order to balance better. The body already balances perfectly. It does this on its own without direction from the mind. We want to feel the body balancing to feel the changes taking place in our body in order to balance. This balancing takes place when I lift a suitcase or any object. My body knows exactly what it needs to do to maintain balance. In the same way, when someone enters my sphere and effects my balance, my body knows exactly how to regain or restore balance. This is a function of my body. This is my natural ability. We all have this ability. The person who walks the tightrope also uses this very same ability. He did not learn a particular way to move across the tightrope. Instead, he cultivated this natural ability of not falling down to such an extent that he could balance on a tightrope between the towers of the World Trade Center. This is not a skill one learns. This is a natural ability of the human body that one cultivates through a practice of awareness. That is the distinction. The process is not cumulative. Rather, it is a stripping away of everything that is unnecessary, a letting go of everything I have learned to discover what is. I am already perfect. I balance perfectly. Let me discover the natural abilities of my body, not just the potential, but the actual abilities. What is present here and now I take for granted, like water for fish.

## Harmonizing

The practice is one of awareness. I am becoming aware of balance, of not falling down within my own body. This is a bodily felt sensation. We have this sensation all of the time (because we are not falling down), yet we choose not to bring attention to it. This natural capacity to balance, to stand up and not fall down, has allowed us to evolve as human beings. We no longer need our arms and hand to balance and to move. They are now available to express our hearts. The problem is that our hearts have not evolved. Our hands and arms now express our lack of love – our fear, our hate and our anger.

We can only bring forth what is inside of us. This is what we seek to discover in standing. We seek to discover what is in our hearts, our *yi*, our heartfelt desire. This is what is expressed in our art. Our art is an expression, a manifestation of what is in our hearts. What is it that is in our hearts? Is it compassion? Is it a longing for oneness or a desire to dominate and control? That is the question we need to ask ourselves. What do we seek? Seek ye first the kingdom of heaven. The kingdom of heaven is within. So what we are seeking, what we are looking for, is within ourselves. We seek to know ourselves, to know our own nature. What is a human being? There are many kinds of being. We want to know what it is to be human, to be of the earth. We want to reach up and out toward heaven. Our desire for oneness, for union, guides us.

We seek to know ourselves intimately in and through our bodies, to feel ourselves, to experience our connection to the earth. We are in harmony with heaven and earth. This is a bodily felt experience. We experience (feel) what it is to be in harmony with the forces of nature. We experience what it is to be in harmony with the magnetic force of gravity drawing us ever closer to the earth. We allow that force. And out of that comes a reaching up toward heaven. We are the harmony of these two forces, a sinking down and a rising up. This is who we are.

There is nothing to achieve or attain, nothing to improve. We are already it. We are the great accomplishment. We seek to know ourselves as we are – our natural capacity. What is the nature of human beings? It is simply shifting our awareness from outside to inside, seeking to know ourselves as we are, as God created us. This is the practice of awareness, a study of intent. What do we want? What do we desire? To be one. To know ourselves as we are instead of what we have been told to believe about ourselves. Separating lies from truth. Not believing anything until you experience it for yourself.

We take so much for granted, like a fish does water. We turn our attention to that. We become aware that, through no effort of our conscious mind, we are able to balance. I don't need to do it, to make it happen. It is already happening. The body balances. The body does not fall down. The body finds harmony with the force of nature all on its own, without any direction from my conscious mind. It is this natural capacity to harmonize with the forces of nature that I seek to cultivate through my practice. I don't resist it or try to overcome it. I allow it.

## Equilibrium Is an Awareness

I am not interested in learning a set of movements. I'm interested in what allows movement, in what is essential to movement – any movement. When the tightrope walker walked between the World Trade Center towers, he wasn't executing a learned set of movements. He didn't spend his training time perfecting a learned set of movements. No, he learned a set of distinctions. Or, more specifically, he cultivated an awareness of his balance, the lived experience of balance. What does it feel like to be in balance with all of the forces of nature?

We are in balance. The fact is that we don't fall down. Yet we take this experience for granted. We turn our awareness to this. When we do, we find a lot is going on in our bodies to maintain balance. Yet this movement is not directed by the conscious mind. It is not fast enough. This is movement of the involuntary nervous system that is not directed by the mind. This is in opposition to movement of the voluntary nervous system that are learned through repetition. As long as we are simply learning and repeating voluntary movements, we cannot gain access to the involuntary system. It is when we stop all external movement and turn our attention inside that we find natural movement, movement that is not mentally generated. It comes from a deeper source. What is it that has the earth move around the sun? What is it that has my lungs breathe in air and my blood flow through my body? What is it that has the sperm seek to fertilize the egg? This is not my mind. I don't need to make it happen. It is already part of the design.

When I stand, I don't need to consciously balance. My body does whatever it needs to do to maintain my equilibrium. Equilibrium (not falling down) is an awareness that I cultivate. I cultivate the awareness of being in harmony with all of the forces of nature. I don't need to make it happen. I am already in harmony. I seek to protect this experience. I seek to maintain my equilibrium without using excess strength. I am not interested in doing anything to anyone. The system maintains harmony – equilibrium. This is the essence of *taiji*. The system (of which I am a part) is designed to maintain equilibrium. I don't need to interfere. I just need to observe.

So what am I teaching? Surely not a set of movements. I am not teaching anything because your body already knows. I want to give you the opportunity to experience what it feels like to let go and experience that you are still standing, to let go and experience that life still works, that it is not me who is doing it. I am not in control, nor do I need to be. I can relax, let go and surrender. All life has a right to protect itself and, if given the opportunity, it will. When I slip on a banana peel, my body does what it needs to do to not fall down. If attacked, my body will do what it needs to do to protect its life. This is our right. It is this natural process that has been overwritten. We need to connect with it, cultivate it and allow it to function as it was designed to. This is my learning and exploration. Can someone show me how to do this? It's like asking, "Can someone show me how to grow hair and nails?" This makes no sense. It is happening already.

## Vertical Axis

Balance is being able to adapt to changes and maintain our equilibrium. We can't stop what happens. We actually have no control over what happens with others and the world. The question is whether we can adjust. In oneness with all that is, as one aspect changes, we also change. Can we allow that, or are we stuck in a certain position? Do we need to maintain a particular viewpoint, a particular way of seeing things, or can we allow it to change in conversation, in communication with others? When we engage with someone else, can we both leave the engagement feeling better about ourselves, more open, more connected? Can we have this as our goal of engagement? This is a win/win interaction, not a win/lose interaction. Can we acknowledge all of our needs and seek to meet them together?

No more right and wrong. Just less wrong, seeking what is in the best interest of all concerned, speaking feelings and needs. It is not a zero-sum game. It is not that there always needs to be a winner and a loser. This is the context we are calling into question. This is aikido. This is Ueshiba's contribution. We transform from a win/lose situation to a win/win situation. We are not concerned only about our own individual needs. We care about all of us because we recognize we are all one being. We are committed to what is in the best interest of all life. No one and nothing is left out. We don't want to succeed at the expense of anyone or anything. We want what nurtures and protects all life, of which we are also a part.

So we are not just looking out for ourselves. We are looking out for all of us. We realize we are in the same boat and we will either sink or swim together, all of us. So what does it mean to be in balance in our interactions, our engagements, with others? It means not giving up our center, not giving up what we care about, what is most precious to us. We maintain this. We can change our point of view, our position, but not what is deepest in our hearts, not our connection to earth and sky. This is primary. There are many positions, many postures. They all have in common the bodily felt sense of our connection to the earth and sky. This we never give up. This is who we are.

Our connection is primarily to the earth and sky, not to others. In fact, there are no others. The connection to ourselves, to our source, does not come from others. It is uniquely ours. This vertical line, this awareness of verticality, this backbone, allows us to stand up, to be vulnerable, to show our hearts to the world and to open to others on the horizontal axis. We cannot do it without being connected to ourselves, without being connected to the earth and sky. We don't need to establish this connection. It is already present.

# THE NATURAL STATE

*Believe me, you need nothing except to be what you are.*
*You imagine you will increase your value by acquisition.*
*It is like gold imagining than an addition of copper will*
*improve it. Elimination and purification of all that is foreign*
*to your nature is enough. All else is vanity.*

*- Nisargadatta Maharaj*

## The Natural State

What is the natural state? It is pre-domesticated, pre-cultural human beings. It is human beings free of all systems and beliefs. It is just being. It is what is left when we take away everything we have learned – all of our beliefs about who we are and what we are doing here. The natural state is a state of oneness. Separation only exists in the mind. It is what the Chinese call *wuji*. It is a state of not-two, an undifferentiated state of oneness with our source. It is recognizing we are one with all that is, an expression of God/Goddess/All That Is.

We practice in order to uncover this state. We don't need to nor can we generate this state. The state is not achieved, attained, learned and so forth. It is. It is what is already present, just covered up. We don't see or know it. So we practice to become aware of it, of the state of oneness with all that is. We recognize the state through *fang sung*. We are reclaiming our inheritance. It's like a street person who has a million dollars in his bank account but isn't aware of it, so he is living in poverty. The natural state is our inheritance. It is who we are, yet we have lost our awareness of it. It has been covered up. Or our eye – our third eye – has become calcified. We cannot see within. We cannot see who or what we are until we begin to question everything we have been told. We believe we are skin encapsulated, separate individuals, separate from each other and from nature. It is this belief, this way of perceiving the world, that hides the truth from us. It is, as Don Juan says, a fixation of the assemblage point. It is a particular way of seeing the world, a particular perspective no one ever questions. Instead, we believe this is the way the world is – not the way we have made it.

So we turn our attention, our awareness, to what is, to the bodily felt sensation of standing up and not falling down. We don't do it. We are held up. We are balanced. We exist in harmony with all that is. In the natural state, all is balanced. Balance is an expression of the natural state. In knowing our own balance intimately we become aware of the natural state. We don't make balance happen. It already is. We are blessed with balance. It is our birthright. We come to know it, to savor it: the earth in balance, human beings in balance with nature. This is the gift that we have been given. This is grace.

## Allowing Change

We stand in order to reveal the natural state. The natural state is what we are. It is pre-cultural. It is undomesticated human beings. It is who we were as humans prior to society, as animals living in the wild. What does that mean? It is the difference between a lion in the wild and a house cat. That undomesticated, wild human is still present. It has been covered over with everything we have learned. What is the nature of wild human beings? What is the nature of undomesticated human beings?

We stop doing. Anything we do is in the world of domesticated human beings. Any action we take is acting in the world of domesticated human beings. Where we discover undomesticated human beings is in our bodily felt sensations. The nature of life for undomesticated humans is the unknown. All life is change, the interplay of yin and yang. Can we feel these changes in our own bodies? The changes are the changes in balance, in equilibrium. Balance is retained. That is the nature of this place – constant change. The path forward is unknown. All I know is that the balance, the equilibrium, is retained. Can I change? Am I willing to? Can I be like water? Water changes when it hits obstacles. It goes around them.

The first step is to stop. Stop doing. Stand. Stand to know yourself from the inside. Stand to know your balance, this play of yin and yang. This operates in me. This is the natural state. I turn my attention to this. Can I allow for change? Or do I see everything from an either/or point of view? I will either be on top or on bottom, and I must be on top. I must dominate so I can control my reality. Rather than learning how to move with change, how to move my feet and keep my equilibrium, I will guard this physical spot. I will hold on to this position and not allow anything to move me. I confuse being balanced with maintaining this particular posture. This couldn't be further from the truth.

The question is, what posture is called for in this situation – not with my mind, but with my body? The posture is only held for as long as is necessary. I am not attached to any posture, any position. I allow myself to change, to evolve. What is constant is balance, my equilibrium. All of the changes in form are meant to maintain the equilibrium. The equilibrium is the natural state. It is being in balance, being one, with all that is. I bring my attention to my balance, to my being in harmony with the force of gravity. I am not falling down. I am not consciously doing it. I am not consciously balancing and yet I am in balance. What is the bodily felt experience of being in balance? I have that experience; I am simply choosing to pay attention to it. This balancing is the natural state. It is already present. I don't need to create it. I simply allow it. I turn my attention to it. I balance. I stand up and don't fall down. I can change positions in any way I need to in order to maintain my equilibrium.

## Returning to the Origin

The practice is about revealing the natural state and my natural ability. It is about revealing who God created me to be, not who I made myself. It's not about gaining or perfecting skill. It is not about getting better. It is about uncovering my true nature. It's not just about seeing myself as energy. It is about knowing myself as source energy. It is knowing I am a manifestation of source energy. That source energy never dies. Life never dies. Yes, it changes its expression of itself. But the energy never dies. I don't need to change myself. I don't need to remake or improve myself. I simply need to know myself as God sees me, as God created me, prior to language and socialization. I need to know my humanness, to love myself simply because I am part of this great mystery. Competition and domination are based on the idea that there are two or more competing factors. There are not two. There is one creation of which we are all part.

We are busy improving this self. Yet this self we are improving is not real. It is socially created. We are working on a socially created self. Drop that self and discover who you really are. It is a discovery, an inquiry into who I am. I don't know who I am. I have mistaken and misidentified myself. I think I need to make myself stronger, faster, more skillful. I don't need to, nor can I, do anything of the kind. The world God created is perfect. It is perfect as it is. We don't need to fix or improve it. We simply need to experience and love it. My ideals are just that – ideals. I am interested in the truth. I am interested in what is real and eternal. Where I look for this is not outside; it is inside. I need to turn my attention within to discover myself.

*Zhan Zhuang*, or standing practice, is about this. I turn my attention from outside to inside and notice what is present. What do I feel in my body? What is actually present here and now? How do I experience that? It is a process of letting go of everything I have been taught and looking at myself and the world with new eyes, the eyes of a child, eyes of wonder and awe. Can I allow myself to be moved and touched by what I feel? Can I allow my heart to open?

I only practice to become what I am, to know what I am. I cannot change or improve what I am. When I know myself as I am, I see there is nothing to improve. Yes, the tree grows. Everything grows. This is not because there is something wrong with the sapling or because the sapling needs to improve itself. The child grows also. This growth process – this process of change – is what life is. I don't need to make it happen. I only need to allow it. It is an expansion of who I am. It is the sharing of who I am. It is the fruit of the tree. The fruiting naturally happens at the right time. I cannot make the fruiting happen – it only happens when the tree is mature. My job is to create an environment in which the tree can grow. I make sure it gets enough sun, water, nourishment and love. And then the tree naturally grows. If it is an apple tree, it will produce apples. I cannot make it a pear tree. Nor would I want to. It is about getting to know myself.

So this is not skill building. That is not the point of this practice. The point is to return to the point of origin, to return to my original nature before the wool was pulled over my eyes. To return to before I bought into this cultural interpretation of everything. To simply be present with what is, seeing myself and the world with the eyes of God.

## Willingness to Change

We stand in order to recover the natural state. What is the natural state? It is change and the unknown. Our whole society is built around dealing with change and the unknown. The fear of change and the unknown is what drives us to predict, manipulate and control our environment. But what if there is another way? What if we don't need to control ourselves, each other and the environment? What if we can change with the changes in the environment? In effect, this is what we do. As our environment changes we also change. Human beings and their environment are one system. The natural ability is to change or adapt. The shape of our body changes, yet we remain in balance. The system is designed to continue. It is always changing – yin becomes yang and yang becomes yin. This is the nature of life. We don't know where it is going – the future is unknown. What we can count on is that it will remain in balance. It is our unwillingness to change our shape that has us lose our equilibrium. I think that in order to maintain balance I must be rooted to this particular place, but I am not a tree. Human beings are designed to move. It is in the willingness to change shape that my equilibrium is maintained. Change is happening anyway. This willingness to change with the changes is my natural ability. It is what has allowed human beings to thrive on this planet. We have populated the entire planet because of our ability to adapt. It is this natural ability that we seek to cultivate.

The natural state is the Tao. It is change and the unknown. It is our willingness to be present in the face of the unknown, to allow change. We don't resist the seasons. We recognize them and appreciate their beauty. This change is happening all the time. We see it in night and day, in summer and winter. It is always happening. Nothing is static. Nothing stays the same. There is movement and change, but not movement and change that I initiate. All things are born, grow and die. That is the nature of this place. It doesn't make sense to resist it. Yet we do resist change in our lives. We want life to stay the same, or we have some idea of how it ought to go, and we try to make it go that way. That is the problem with practicing techniques. What is the purpose of practicing a particular attack and technique? *Uke* and *nage* are one system, not two. As *uke* changes, *nage* changes. If we are one, then we evolve together as one system. I don't need to learn how to respond to the changes in your body. I just need to be present and willing to evolve with you. This willingness is the natural ability we wish to cultivate. If I don't resist you, then there is no fight. So I am practicing nonresistance, maintaining my equilibrium by not resisting anything. I simply am present and available. That is the practice.

## The Energy Protects

All animals naturally protect themselves. If they are attacked, they defend themselves and their loved ones. Even a cockroach will attempt to preserve its own life. They require no training or technique to do this. It is innate in them. It is part of their God-given program. So why do we, as human beings, think we need to train to defend ourselves? Why do we need to study martial arts or learn particular movement patterns?

We, as human beings, also have our natural function, but it has been covered up by everything we have been taught about who we are and what life is. The process is not about learning techniques, movement patterns or skills to overcome others. We don't need any of this. This was Wang Xiang Zhai's contribution. Instead, we need to uncover the natural state we share with all animals and all life. *Qi* will protect itself. It is designed that way. All animals have natural defenses. The armadillo will roll up into a ball. The scorpion will sting. We don't need to learn new skills and techniques. Instead, we need to reconnect with the natural state. We need to reconnect with what is. We need to reconnect with our self. We do this through the body. We do this through coming into the present moment and feeling our bodies. We connect with *qi*.

The purpose of the practice is to become increasingly aware of the natural state, the state of human beings prior to domestication. We wipe the computer clean of all of its learned programs. How do we do this? We do this by ceasing to act, ceasing to think, ceasing to achieve. We simply are. And in this being-ness we discover our natural state. We discover what it is to be a human being, not a human doing. Our natural ability is to care for *qi*. It is in our relationship with *qi* that all things are healed and resolved. We seek to cultivate an awareness of this energy and to allow it to move freely in and through us. The unrestricted flow of *qi* is the essence of healing and of protecting life. We seek to melt any blockages to *qi* that we are aware of in our bodies. This usually shows up as some form of contraction in our musculature, what Reich called "armoring." This armoring seeks to hold the current patterns in place. When we practice *fang sung*, we are letting go and releasing all musculature, all contraction that is not necessary to stand up and not to fall down.

We are interested in discovering our natural state. We are interested in discovering who we were prior to what we have been told. Perhaps we are not who or what we have been told we are, We need to be scientists and discover this for ourselves, to discover what it is to be a human being. We are not interested in adding anything to who or what we are. We are interested in letting go of everything that is not true. We no longer accept what we have been told. It is time to find out for ourselves the truth of our own being. What is that? We discover this in stillness. We stop all action, all thinking and all doing and discover the essence of who we are. We allow it to be. We allow it to speak. We allow it full expression in and through our bodies. We allow it to manifest according to its own desire. It desires to express and be known, and we surrender to and allow that.

# MOVEMENT

*Movement is what we are, not something we do.*

*- Emilie Conrad*

## External versus Internal Movement

External movement is generated by the voluntary nervous system. I use *li*, physical effort. I watch someone perform a movement and then attempt to replicate it. I see a beautiful piece of artwork and I copy it. Internal movement is different. I don't need to make the movement happen. I need to discover the preexisting movement within myself, the involuntary movement my body is engaged in moment to moment in order to maintain its own equilibrium. How do you teach someone balance? You don't say, "Put your foot here and put your hand there." No, it's about discovering internally – feeling and sensing what it feels like to be balanced. I don't need to make balance. Balance exists. Harmony exists. When I stand up, I am in balance with the forces of gravity. The system is designed to be in balance. My body knows how to maintain equilibrium. It is a master at not falling down already. I seek to expand this natural capacity – to bring it into more challenging situations and environments.

What is the right way to move? How should I move? Move in a way that feels good. Move in a way that maintains your equilibrium. This is natural movement. We do this already. It does not need to be taught. Let go of any programmed movements. We are wiping the hard drive clean and returning to the original operating system. You see, many of the programs that have been installed are simply unnecessary. Do I need to teach my body to pull my hand back when I touch a hot stove? There is no correct movement. The correct movement is the one that is effective. My body already knows how to take my hand away. Instead, I want to become more sensitive. What if I can feel the heat sooner? What if I don't actually need to touch the hot stove to know that it is hot and that I need to move my hand away? This is internal practice.

It is not about copying other people's movements. The movement needs to originate from the heart. I want to be free to move in whatever way feels good to me. I do not want to be constrained. That's why my *sifu* said: "You do yours; I do mine." I can never do your movement. What's important here is listening to the movement within. To listen I need to be still. I need to stop all voluntary movement and listen to the movement within. What is it saying? How does it want to move? What does it feel like to move?

In the stillness I find the universal movement. I discover *qi* moving in and around me. It is this that I am interested in. This is my teacher and I surrender myself to this energy. I surrender my body to the *qi* within. I feel it and I say yes. This *qi* will protect itself. It is in harmony with all that is. It is the source of all that is. It was present before this body appeared and will be present after it is gone. I am experiencing, experimenting and playing with this *qi*, allowing it to move in whatever way it wants and needs to move. I will not inhibit it.

## Internal Movement

The movements do not matter. The only question I have is whether this particular gesture expresses what is in your heart. Is it expressive? Does it convey something, or is it the imitation of an external movement? The external movement arises from an internal experience. We make the internal experience visible in the world through our movement. It is not just a physical movement. It is an expression of something deeper. How do we access that something deeper? We access it not through movement, but through stillness. By not doing we return our attention to what is present here and now. That is who we are. We allow whatever movement is present to just be. We give it space and we allow it to expand and grow and to express itself through us. It is the internal movement itself that finds expression through us.

It is movement for movement's sake. It is not about achieving anything. It is not about stopping anything. Life moves naturally – the waves, the planets, sperm. It is all movement in harmony with itself. We are a part of that movement of life. We allow that movement and we experience it. It is a movement toward wholeness, toward oneness. It is a joining. We need to do nothing other than to allow ourselves to know this movement. We allow it to touch us, to transform us, to heal us. We allow the movement of *qi* through our bodies.

This is why *fang sung* is so important. To allow the movement, we need to let go. We need to stop trying to control anything and simply allow what is to be. We allow the movement of *qi* in us. We know this is a movement toward wholeness. The energy flows through all life. It is one energy, not separate energies. It is the energy of life and we allow it to move.

## No Forms

What if every conversation we had with someone needed to follow a certain protocol? This would get very boring after a while. Once we get to know someone and trust them, we can share with each other from our hearts. We can express ourselves to each other authentically. We can see we are actually the same. Much of our authentic expression is not allowed in life. We need to behave in certain ways, live a certain way, think certain things and so forth. The beauty of this practice is that we let all of that go. We drop it and tune in to what is alive in us, our own energy – or, more accurately, *qi*. I don't need to know what I am going to do before I actually do it. There are no set forms. There are only natural responses in the moment. I free myself up to allow what needs to come forth to do so. To write, we need to learn the alphabet. We need to learn words. Yet what is beautiful about writing is the infinite ways in which we can combine words. It is not the words that matter, not the notes that are played or the paint strokes on the canvas that matter. It is what is in our hearts that is revealed through our expression.

My movements are not about doing something to you. Nor are they simply about defending myself. My movements reveal my heart. They are a manifestation of what is inside me. I want the space to express this. Yes, I need to learn the alphabet, but after a time, after I have learned it, I want to write words, sentences and paragraphs and use the language to manifest, to express what is deep within. I don't want to write someone else's sentences. I want it to be brand-new in the moment, a unique expression never seen before and never seen again, born out of nothing and returning to nothing. I am the stillness out of which movement is born. The wind stirs and there is natural movement. My body loves to move, easily and naturally, with nowhere to go and nothing to achieve. There is simply the joy of movement with another until there is no me and you – there is only the movement, the expression of love.

## Surrendering Voluntary Movement

The tendency is to look outside of ourselves for approval. We want others to validate what we are doing. Yet in looking for approval we give away our own innate sense of knowing. We are saying others know more than we do about how we ought to be moving, as if there is some right way of moving that shows up externally. We are always focused on how it looks, its external manifestation. I am proposing that we pay attention to how it feels to us. Just because we get the external form to look a certain way, it means nothing. This culture is totally focused on externals: how things look, what others think. I am questioning the whole idea that others can show us how we ought to live or how we want to move. I am speaking of movement that is totally free. It is not predetermined. This is not a *kata* – a set movement pattern that we are practicing. We are surrendering voluntary movement. We stop moving. We stop doing. We simply be. We release. We let go. We *fang sung*. We are not concerned with external movement. We are concerned with accessing the natural state, which is free of all forms and of all intent. It is simply being.

There are no magical movement patterns. We are not interested in ritual. We are interested in spontaneous, creative, free movement, and in accessing and allowing this movement – this true movement. This is not movement to produce some effect, but movement simply for the joy of it. This movement is happening all the time below the level of our consciousness. We seek to make it conscious.

Gaia is a self-regulating system. It is working in our bodies as well. The system seeks balance. It is resilient. We as humans can adapt.

This capacity to change, to transform, is key. We are nonresistant. We can go from day to night and back to day, from summer to winter and back to summer. This is life. It is not static. This is breathing. There is inhale and exhale, both part of the same process, two sides of the same coin. There is movement and stillness, tension and relaxation, and the capacity to move between these two. We seek to free this capacity to change.

## Heavenly Movement

I want to remove the illusion that there is something for me to do, some result for me to produce, some technique for me to perform. I am not trying to accomplish anything. How could anything that I produce come close to the miracle that I am? That we are? The idea that my job as *nage* is to do something to *uke* is preposterous. My job is simply to maintain my own equilibrium. That is all. This does not depend on doing anything to you. The system is designed to seek balance. It is this system that I seek to cultivate by bringing my attention to it. I recognize it. I become aware of how it works naturally. This wisdom of the body does not depend on conscious control. I can't make it happen. It is already happening. Any learning of movement patterns simply conceals the natural function of the human operating system – or, better yet, the Gaian operating system.

It is a question of uncovering what is already there. We seek to become aware of our natural ability – balancing. We seek to allow this to function unimpeded in our life. The system desires to return to balance, always seeking the continuance of the play. In an infinite game, we are not concerned with winning and losing. We are concerned with the continuance of play. There is nowhere to get to. What is not is not more important than what is. The fact is that we don't need to learn anything. We don't need to improve ourselves or make ourselves better than what we already are. We simply desire to know ourselves as bipedal primates, the only animals that balance on two legs. This capacity allows us to use tools and makes us uniquely human. We seek to know this natural ability and to cultivate it.

We cultivate through awareness, by allowing it to grow. We can't make it grow. Growth is part of life. So we stop doing things that get in the way of the functioning of our natural ability. Set movement patterns get in the way, looking at someone's external manifestation and then copying it. Revealed in the world is a physical expression of what is in our heart. It is the physical manifestation of a feeling. This is art. It expresses who we are. We can't fake it. The movement means nothing if it doesn't originate from within, from a feeling. The movement is a sharing – a making visible of what is invisible. The movement begins from within – natural movement. The movement is designed to maintain equilibrium. This is true movement. I don't produce it. I only allow it. This is the movement of life as it expresses through my body, heavenly movement.

# AWARENESS

*When attention is directed toward objects and intellect, the mind is aware only of these things. That is our present state of suffering. But when we attend to the self within, we become conscious of it alone. It is therefore all a matter of attention.*

**- Ramana Maharshi**

## Energy Never Dies

This art is about the free expression of *qi* through me, through this body. It has nothing to do with movement. It has nothing to do with others at this point. It is simply my surrender to the free flow of *qi*. The art is an art of awareness of *qi*, of source energy, of that energy that causes the tree in my front yard to blossom with beautiful white flowers, the little green sprouts to show up, the grass to grow. This is the energy of life. This energy also exists within me. It is what circulates my blood and makes me breathe. We seek to connect with this energy, and we do this through stillness. By not doing anything, by ceasing all movement, we turn our attention within. We pay attention to our bodily felt sensations. This is where life energy shows up. We may not see it, hear it, smell it, touch it or taste it, but we can feel it. We can feel it and we can allow it. We can let it be. We can be curious about it.

Anything we are doing interferes with this awareness. We are not driving the car. We are the passenger. *Qi* is driving the car. Any system is a prison. No one can tell us how we ought to move, how we ought to respond to a situation. We are way too reliant on outside experts. It is because we don't trust our internal GPS. It is about allowing this energy to lead, to move us, to direct us. We open to it. We let go, *fang sung*. We release it all into the earth and we are an empty vessel, available, open. Form? No form. Intent? No intent. Just open. Just available. Listening. We discover there is an energy present, an intelligent energy that is active, moving, expressive. It has something to share. It is speaking to us. We allow it to move us. It is moving already. We simply choose to allow it and to participate in its movement. Its movement is the movement of planets around the sun, the movement of the waves, the rain, the sun. It is a natural movement, the movement of electrons and protons, all the time. This movement seeks expression through us. This is the movement of life. What does this movement look like? There is no set form. It is balanced and it is not effortful. That is all I can say. It is also whole movement. The movement occurs through the entire system. We as human beings have been blocking that movement with our systems, our way of doing things, our ideas of right and wrong. We have blocked it by mistaking what we have made for what is real. The only thing that is real is this movement. When all has passed, what will remain is the movement of *qi*, the dance and play of energy. Forms are transitory. *Qi* is eternal. Energy never dies. It has no beginning and no end. Are you interested, curious? We seek true movement in stillness, the movement of *qi* that sourced you and me and all we see. We cannot, we dare not, tell this energy how to express. We can only point to it, open to it, allow it. We don't need to make it. We can't. It was here long before you and I showed up and will exist long after we pass. It is eternal.

## Know Yourself

The practice is not about adding skill. In fact, it is not about adding anything. It is about bringing awareness to what already is. We are interested in stillness and movement: not the movement of muscles, not movement controlled by the mind, but movement initiated prior to the mind. Spontaneous movement. True movement. This is movement to maintain equilibrium. This is our natural ability, our natural function. We don't need to learn how to move this way. Our body already knows. We are seeking to know this movement. Or, shall I say, we are seeking the manifestation of this movement as it expresses itself through our human bodies. The movement is the same – the movement of the earth around the sun, the movement of the waves, the movement of the clouds and the movement of our bodies to maintain balance. These are all manifestations of the Tao, of nature. This movement is discovered in stillness. It is discovered when we cease all mentally generated movement and come into stillness. In the space of stillness we discover a movement that we are not consciously creating. We are interested in the bodily felt experience of this movement. We surrender to this movement and allow it to move in and through us.

We are not creating this movement. It is happening. We allow it. We are nonresistant to the movement of life as it expresses itself in and through us. The movement is a balancing movement that enables us to stand up and not fall down. This allows us to no longer use our hands to balance and frees them to use tools. It allows us to evolve and realize our genetic potential. It is a movement whose intent is to join and to restore balance, to restore equilibrium to the entire system by bringing movement to all of the stuck places. The movement itself has the intent of harmony, of standing up and not falling down, of full self-expression. We are interested in bringing our awareness to this movement.

Tsuda calls it the regenerative movement. It is the movement of *qi* through the system. It regenerates. It brings life. Movement is life. It is the physical manifestation of Goddess, of all that is. We welcome and are open to the movement of life. This welcoming and opening is what we call *fang sung*. Only in this state of release can we experience the regenerative movement. Therefore, the first step is *sung*, relaxation and release, letting go. We stand to know the natural state. Only through *fang sung* can the natural state be known.

## Accessing Innate Knowing

These days, we can't seem to do anything without an expert. We have lost all confidence in our own inner knowing. Animals don't need experts. They instinctively know what they need to do. They naturally give birth. A cat knows to eat grass when its stomach is upset. Who told it to do this? Did it consult with the vet? We human beings have lost touch with what is natural to us. The most natural act – giving birth – now requires an expert. All animals, even insects, defend themselves when their life is threatened. Yet why do we human beings feel we need to learn how to defend ourselves? We have lost touch with our own innate knowing, so we look outside for answers.

Yiquan is not about learning new skills. It is not about learning anything. It is about recovering the natural state of the undomesticated human being and accessing the knowledge that has guided us since the beginning. We have been taught that we know nothing, that we are nothing, that we have no worth and no value other than what we can produce. This is the lie of capitalism. All our attention goes outward. We are always looking outside of ourselves for knowledge, never within. Why? Perhaps it's a little like opening a dark room that has been closed for many, many years. Who knows what lives in there? Stay away from that room. Never open that door.

What we are interested in, what we are committed to, is recovering the natural state. The natural state is present already, underneath all of our learning, our habits, our beliefs and the lies we have been told. We wipe it all clean. We let go of all of this external programming and discover what is actually present. Human beings have managed to stay alive and to thrive. What allowed this? It is our own innate knowing. Just as all animals know what they need to do to survive, so do we as human beings know this. Yet we have overridden our own internal knowing. We are no longer listening to ourselves. If we listened to ourselves, it might require us to change our behavior. We would need to stop poisoning and destroying the environment. We would care for all of us, for each other and for the life on this planet as true family. We would need to stop doing the things we are doing. We do not want to change, so we do not go within.

*Yiquan* is a practice of going within. Yes, there are movements. The movements are not *yiquan*. Rather, *Yiquan* is about where we place our attention. Energy follows attention. We turn our attention within. We pay attention to the bodily felt sense. This is what we have lost our connection to – how we feel in our bodies. We declare that this matters. This is important. We allow our feelings to lead our movement, to lead all our action. This is *yiquan*. It is the bodily felt sense that contains the wisdom of millions of years of life on this planet. Would we turn away from this? We seek to reconnect with this knowing that has guided our race for millennia. We allow this to guide our movement, not someone else telling us how to move, how to breathe and so forth. How do they know? What is the source of their knowing? Oh, the founder knows, and he passed it down to his student, who passed it down to his student, who passed it down to you.

Yet how does the founder know? We are interested in how to access this innate knowing within ourselves. The direction arises from within.

## Attention

We came here to be in a body, so let's experience it. We turn our attention within. Always our attention goes out into the world and we pretend this is the only world. The inner world is a world of bodily felt sensations. We turn our attention to these and drop any story that is connected. We are simply present with what we are experiencing – going deeper into it. It is pure sensation with no story attached. That is what we are after. In stillness, what is present presents itself to us. Much of what we do in the world is an attempt to avoid feeling. We try to distract ourselves, to get away from it, because it is not comfortable. This is no longer necessary. We stop turning away and turn toward. It is like comforting an upset child – we are present for her with open arms.

We are looking to connect – to contact this feeling, whatever it is. As we pay attention to it, it changes and transforms. It is not just one thing. It is our inner life, our feeling life – some would say our intuition – our inner knowing. It is always present. We simply turn our attention there. We turn our attention to what is happening inside our body/mind. Something is happening. We are not doing it. It is already there. It is a feeling – a sensation. Life is speaking to us and we are now listening. What is life saying? What is being communicated? We turn down the external noise so we can hear it. What is it saying? Don't pretend you already know. Listen.

We tune into our internal state. We redirect our attention from external to internal. Whatever our art is, it is born from within ourselves, from this inner sensation, this bodily felt experience. We give it space and allow it to speak. It speaks to us through sensations. It speaks to us through internal movement, through the movement of *qi*. We allow it. We are simply discovering what it is that is present. What is this energy, this force, that gives birth to us? What is this evolutionary force that has man stand on two feet and balance? This force operates within us and we seek to know it, to feel it and experience it. We allow it to carry us. We surrender to it, to this energy that has the earth rotate, that has the planets move around the sun, that has birds migrate, that makes birthing happen. This force is operating in and through us and we seek to surrender to it.

Don't think. Just be. There is nothing to figure out, nothing to arrive at. There is nowhere to go, nothing to achieve. We can't make the trees grow. We can only provide good soil, sunlight and water. That is our job. We don't make the growing happen. We don't make our own inner growing happen either. We allow it. We support it. We create an environment in which we can turn our attention within. We stop doing. We stop achieving. We are simply present, breathing, feeling, experiencing the *qi* within. We are not trying to harness it or do anything with it. We are surrendering to it, allowing it to move through all parts of our body. This energy returns us to our source. This energy is our source. This is who we are. We seek to know ourselves as energy, as that which is prior to our identity, the pure *qi* that flows through our bodies, that animates us. Can we know this? Are we willing to experience this? We don't need to make it; it is already here. We simply choose to turn our attention away from the world and focus on that which animates us.

## Three Treasures

*Jing, qi* and *shen* are known as the three treasures in Taoism. They are not separate. Just as ice, water and vapor are three forms of H2O, so *jing, qi* and *shen* are three forms of life energy. As we increase heat, ice becomes water and eventually vapor. As we increase our own heat, our *jing* transforms to *qi* and *qi* becomes *shen*. So first of all, *jing, qi* and *shen* are phases in the cultivation of life force energy. We start with *jing*. *Jing* is the vital life force we have been given. It is what separates a live body from a dead body. We apply heat to it. What is heat? It is our attention, our awareness. We focus our awareness on the *jing*. As we do so, the *jing* becomes more refined. Our awareness transforms the *jing* to *qi*. It is not just physical energy. It is not just the fact that we are alive.

When we turn our attention to our life force energy and allow this energy to rise from the earth up our spine, it begins to open our hearts. We feel the life force around us. We see that what animates us animates all life. This life force energy is *qi*. It is not just inside of us. It is all around us. We feel connected. We are open to giving and receiving life force energy. We share our life force energy with others. We give and receive love. We feel love for the earth and for our brothers and sisters. As we continue to cultivate it, we realize we are all connected. As we continue to place our focus on life force energy and allow it to rise up our spines into our head, we are awakened. We see and know our true self. We see ourselves and everything as one energy expressed in a myriad of forms. We are no longer blinded by the illusion of separation. By focusing on vital life force, we come to see that this is our source and the source of everything we see. We begin to know this life force energy as who we are. Our eyes are opened. We no longer see separation. We know all is one. This is the cultivation of life force energy. The heat we apply is our minds, our *yi*. We place our attention on the vital life force within our own bodies. This attention allows the vital life force energy to become more refined. You could say that, as we pay attention to vital life force energy, our awareness becomes more refined. We feel things that we could not feel before. Distinctions we did not have before allow us to be present with vital life force energy in a way that simply was not possible before.

The transformation of *jing* is a natural process. We don't need to do anything to make it happen. It is when we stop doing and just be present that our attention naturally rests in our vital life force energy. It is a process of letting go. Ice does not struggle to become water and vapor. It happens naturally when we apply heat and light. We are simply directing heat and light to our vital life force energy and noticing the transformation, the refinement of our energy. The energy naturally rises. That is what it does. It cannot rise if the channels are blocked. That is why *fang sung* is the doorway. We need to relax and release before we can allow ourselves to be filled with life force energy. We release everything we have been holding on to, not just physical tension. We release old beliefs, old ways of interpreting the world. We also release our fear and hatred, our desire to seek revenge. We just let it all go. We are being held in the arms of the Great Mother and we relax and give all of our concerns to her. She gladly receives them and holds them. This is our outbreath, a full outbreath. And now we naturally inhale the love of the earth for us. We inhale her energy, her support and her life-giving force, and we allow it to rise. It rises to our hearts where we feel deep love and gratitude for being alive and connected. As it continues to rise, it opens our third eye. We come to know ourselves as we are, as one with all that is, an expression of vital life force energy. We see the emptiness of all form, the nothing-ness of everything we see. We see that who we thought we are does not even exist. It is a mental construction. We realize that all is empty inside and out. We merge with and become the emptiness. This is the natural transformation of *jing*.

# SOURCE ENERGY

*There is a force within which gives you life – seek that.*

*- Rumi*

## Grace

"Return to the origin." What does that mean? It means return to the source. We recognize that we are not separate from all that is. In fact, there is only one. All separation is in the mind. There is no separation. There never was. We have been led to believe we are separate individuals, separate from each other and all we see. Any art that comes out of separation will involve manipulation and control of the other. We stand in order to return to the source, to the origin. *Wu*. It means emptying ourselves of everything that is not who we are, releasing all beliefs and culturally programmed ways of perceiving the world, to be eaten by Mother Earth.

We are received and held by Mother Earth. We don't see it or acknowledge it, but it is so. We are in relationship with the earth and the sky. Without Mother Earth, we would not be alive. She provides us with everything we need without asking anything in return. She gives it to us and all living beings because we are her children and she loves us. We don't see it and don't recognize how we are held and nurtured by Mother Earth. She is at the root. Without her, there is no life. It is this life-giving force that we recognize. We receive the life given to us with gratitude. We have all been endowed with life, with a part of the Mother. It is this life force within us that we seek to cultivate, to come to know. This life force is grace, it is a gift we receive with appreciation. We seek to nourish and nurture this life force in ourselves, each other and our environment.

We create space for this life force energy to flow. We recognize and appreciate this flow of life force energy: one flow in, through and all around us. We participate in the flow of life force energy, source energy. It is this source energy that heals and transforms. It is inside us and our job is simply to turn our attention to it. The path is to begin to see and feel this life force energy. This becomes the sole object of our concentration. We find that it is alive – it is life itself. We allow this energy to have its way in and through us. We surrender to it. We let it move. We no longer seek to control and manipulate it. It has its own intelligence, its own way.

In fact, we discover that this is the only thing that is real. All forms shall pass, yet the energy remains. We allow the changing manifestations. We allow the free flow of life force energy. We open to it, *fang sung*. We must relax, release and open, letting go of everything we know, giving it all to Mother Earth. It is the desire to return home to the source that matters. Trust this desire. Feel it in your heart and allow it to lead you back to your true self. It is this desire to know ourselves and to know God that matters.

## Already Connected

The connection is internal. In fact, we are already connected to everything and everybody. We are connected because we are part of one system. We are connected to the system in the same way the mycelium connects fruiting bodies. I don't need to make a connection. I don't need to do anything. I only need to become aware of the life force energy flowing though me. *Yi* precedes *qi*. My desire to join, for God, for love, opens me to receiving life force energy. I need to create space in my heart for love. I don't want to walk around all day being shut off. It is like my home; I don't want to create walls, moats and locks. I also don't want my doors and windows wide open. This requires discrimination. When I meet someone and they stick out their hand to me, is this an act of friendship or an attack? I need to be present. I need to be open. I want to be free to respond to each and every situation uniquely. It is one system. As the system changes, I change. I resist nothing. I allow. I change with the changes. I am not trying to do anything, nor am I trying to prevent anything. I am present, allowing my body to respond naturally to each and every situation. My job is to drop everything and simply be in the moment.

I am already connected to all that is. We all come from the same source. Whatever created you also created me and all that we see. To know this is to know we are one, to know whatever I do affects you and visa versa. We are connected to the earth and to each other. How we choose to live has an effect. It matters. I don't need to establish connection. Connection already exists – I just need to pay attention and be open and willing. I don't connect in order to do something to you. I am connected. I am part of a larger whole. This is really what it is about. It is about identity. It is about who I am versus who I think I am. Question everything. I have been told that I am this individual body that was born and will die. Who does this interpretation serve? I need to realize I am in a virtual reality created by human beings in order to control and dominate other human beings. We have been fed a pack of lies about who we are and what we are doing here. The lies allow us to be controlled and our energy harvested. This is about reclaiming our birthright as energy beings.

We can play with the energy of other energy beings. We can use this play to become aware of ourselves as energy beings. We are simply the play of energy. That is who or what we are. It has nothing to do with protecting ourselves or dominating others. It has to do with adapting. It has to do with cultivating our natural intelligence.

## Purifying Our Heart

We are in a process of purification. What does that mean? It means an alchemical process. We are pure gold that has somehow lost its purity. Or, rather, it has lost the awareness of itself as pure gold. We don't turn lead into gold. Lead is lead and gold is gold. What we do is distinguish between lead and gold. We distinguish between truth and illusion. The truth is that we are pure love. We are not what we think we are. This is what is transformed. What is transformed is our way of seeing. What we have been taught is lead has been gold all along.

We feel the hurt in our own hearts. We don't want to feel it; we don't want to open to it. And yet it is this hurt, this longing for the Mother, for love, that transforms us, that opens our heart. We push the hurt away and yet it is this very hurt that has the power to open our hearts. We would do anything to not feel this pain. This pain may be a sensation in the heart at first. We open to it and allow ourselves to feel this longing. It is this longing that will guide us back to ourselves. We are not trying to change it, heal it or get rid of it. We are simply willing to be present with it, much in the same way that we would be present with a child, loving that child just as they are.

Transformation may happen; however, that is not our goal. We have no goal. We are simply present with what is in our own bodies.

We are present with the bodily felt sense of what is. This may be comfortable, uncomfortable, painful, blissful – all of these things. These are the changes. We simply let them be and offer them our awareness, getting to their essence. We want to feel pure feeling, or, better yet, the pure sensation within our own bodies. The sensations move toward resolution and wholeness. We simply follow the bodily felt sensation with our awareness. We feel it, pay attention to it. It leads us deeper within itself, to its core. Understanding may or may not come. It's not about changing it. Many of us grew up in situations where we were not allowed our feelings. We could only show happiness and everything else was pushed away.

We now give our feelings space. We declare that all feelings are welcome. All feelings contain innate knowing. We are learning how to respect these feelings as sources of knowledge and understanding on a deeper level than our thoughts. The work is being present – fully present – with awareness and compassion. We give up all desire to change what we are feeling. We accept and work with what we are given. We give it space to be, to change and to evolve. It is giving us information about our world. All feelings are valid. Many of our feelings we have had for as long as we remember. Who was there to fully receive us in our pain and hurt? Backed up by Mother Earth, we can now allow ourselves these feelings.

The important thing here is that all feelings are valid. Growing up, we learned some feelings are valid and others are not, but there is no right way to feel. Let's not cut ourselves off from our feeling self. In so doing, we cut ourselves off from our innate knowing. We are reclaiming all aspects of ourselves. We are purifying our hearts, or allowing them to be purified. We purify through awareness and acceptance of all we experience in our hearts.

## A Heart That Cares

Why should we move or breathe according to what someone else tells us we should do? We are interested in connecting with our own innate knowing, the part of us that balances easily and naturally. We are not looking for anyone else to tell us what to do or how to do it. We are opening to our own innate knowing. We are not in control; we have never been. We don't decide when we are born nor do we decide when we die, who our parents are and so forth. We give control of our life to a higher power. We let go. We surrender. We stop thinking we need to direct anything. We are not in the driver's seat. We are in the passenger seat. It's time to allow ourselves to enjoy the ride. There is nowhere we need to go.

Can we simply abide in the here and now? Simply be present and accept this moment exactly as it is? Think of the mother who holds and cares for her infant. We are that infant. We are that new baby that is birthing our true self, holding the space of love for that which needs to die to die and that which needs to be born to be born. We don't get to decide. We are willing to let go of all that is not us, of all illusion, all habits, all routines, all the ways we have figured it out. We let go of our designs and plans. We come back into this present moment and ask what is required. What is my part? It is a willingness to contribute, to be helpful, to do whatever it is that needs to be done with a heart that cares and is compassionate. This is who we are. We seek to know our own heart. We seek to know what it is that we care about most deeply. We seek to know unconditional love. And we seek to know ourselves. What have we given up to be part of this culture? That is a good question to ask.

## Self-Regulating Living Systems

The opportunity of practice is to know ourselves. I have often thought about animals in the wild. Why doesn't a tiger need to practice? He doesn't need to practice because he is already a tiger. If he is attacked, he does whatever he needs to do to defend himself. This is a function of all living systems. All living systems seek to preserve themselves in the face of adversity. They naturally do this. All animals do. It is the same with human beings. We simply need to allow the system to function. We are, each of us, a living system that seeks its own equilibrium. All living systems have a self-regulatory function. The living system will preserve itself through maintaining its equilibrium with its environment. The system is designed to work. We simply need to get out of the way.

When we stand, we are simply allowing our self-regulatory function to operate unimpeded. The earth, Gaia, is also a self-regulating living system. We are allowing that system to work. It is working now. When we look at things, we only see a snapshot in time. And based on that snapshot we think we know what is going on. The fact is that we have no idea what is actually happening here and now. We think we know. We make up all kinds of stories about what is going on. Yet do we really know? What if we acknowledged that we don't have a clue? There is a higher intelligence built into Gaia and we surrender to it. We don't need to know. We don't need to figure it out or fix anything. We simply need to allow it to move. The movement is not generated by the mind. We are tapping into and experiencing a preexistent movement that existed before human beings and will continue after human beings are gone.

We don't need to learn anything except how to let go and surrender. *Fang sung gong.* We don't need to make ourselves better. We simply need to know ourselves as we are, to know the nature of who or what we are as a living system. We naturally seek to preserve ourselves. We don't need to learn techniques or practice to preserve ourselves. This is a natural function of all living systems. We need to stand down, to get out of the way and allow the system to work as it was designed. It doesn't need to be fixed or improved upon. All of our troubles are due to the fact that we have been trying to improve upon the system. We don't even understand who we are, but we want to change and improve upon it.

So we practice – if you want to call it that – to return to an awareness of ourselves as a living system, as part of a larger living system. In other words, it is all alive. It is all one. And we are a part of that one. We seek to let go and surrender to our part in this grand design. We step back and allow ourselves to be guided.

# RESPONSE-ABILITY

*So people who can follow their instincts are much better protected than by all the wisdom of the world.*

*- Carl Jung*

## The Capacity to Change

When I lift a suitcase, my body naturally maintains its balance. When I slip on a banana peel, my body naturally attempts to not fall down. This is not just a function of my body. This is a function of the entire self-regulating system. The system changes. The earth changes. It changes in order to continue to be. If we can't change, we die as a species. If we can't adjust to earth's changes, we die. It is this capacity to change, this resilience, that has allowed human beings to thrive. This is our natural ability that we seek to cultivate in our work.

How do we do it? We do it through awareness. We are doing it all the time. When we are standing, our body is constantly adjusting in order to maintain equilibrium. We bring our attention to these minute changes in our body. We notice them and allow them. It is not our rootedness that allows us to maintain balance. It is our capacity to allow change. Change is already happening all around us. We seek to conserve our equilibrium within these changes. This equilibrium is not a concept. It is a bodily felt sense. We seek to cultivate the bodily felt sense of balance through *zhan zhuang*.

I cannot change the world. I cannot change you. I can, however, allow my body to change in response to yours. If we are one, then as you change, I change. My change is not a reaction to yours. It is one change that manifests in both you and me. I change with you. In fact, there is no you and me. There is only the change, the transformation. There is a flow. I allow that flow. I allow myself to be touched and moved by it. This is very different from trying to maintain my position or my identity. It is like buttressing ourselves against the flow of the river.

The first step, the doorway, so to speak, is *fang sung*. There is no unnecessary tension in my body, mind or heart. My body balances naturally without my mental direction. When we stop doing, when we stop moving, we become aware of this natural ability to stand up and not fall down, to adjust to changes in the environment.

## What Is Freedom?

It is allowing whatever needs to happen to happen, allowing things to evolve and change however they may need to. It is the ability to fully respond in the moment to whatever is happening, free from the constrictions of my mind. I need to just allow my body to respond. I don't need to figure it out. My body is connected and is part of all that is. It will naturally respond to changes and challenges. And this is not by way of my mind. It is pre-interpretive. My participation in life is prelinguistic. There is that which comes before and allows for language. It is the fact that we are one, that we are here and that we love and are loved. We don't learn these things. Existence is not learned; it is only experienced.

I am interested in internal movement: the movement of the flower blooming, the child maturing, the tree growing, the clouds moving across the sky. It is not controlled by my mind. The movement occurs without me having to make it happen. I allow the movement. I allow. I do not resist it. I do not make my own movements. There is a natural movement. This natural movement is life. It is happening now. The earth is circling the sun. Blood is circulating in my system.

So I am not interested in learning external movements. The system already knows how to respond. I slip on a banana peel. Do I need to learn a technique or series of movements to right myself? No, I naturally right myself. Someone sticks out their hand to shake hands. My hand naturally responds. Someone throws a baseball. My hands naturally rise to catch it, unmediated by my mind. What technique is best? The one that uses the least energy and allows me to stay balanced. The body knows. The system knows. Life knows. Life is intelligent.

## Heavenly Movement

I no longer want to do someone else's art. I want to discover my art, whatever that is, beginning in stillness and noticing the natural movement of life within me. It is same movement as the wind, as the clouds, as the rain. I don't cause this movement. This is heavenly movement, not directed by my mind. And yet there is natural movement, the movement of life force energy. This is where the healing and transformation resides – in life force energy. We don't make this energy, rather we are an expression of it. We don't need to figure it out. In fact, we can't. All we can do is to allow.

I am practicing allowing. I am practicing feeling. I am practicing self-awareness. Everything is valid. I am not practicing a set response or particular movements. I am making the equipment more sensitive, more able to respond. Just don't fall down and don't use excess effort. Allow and notice the change within your own body moment to moment. This is life. Allow it. Feel it. Enjoy it. Feel the spirit of God move on the face of the waters. Feel this inside of your own body. Moment by moment. Life. The movement of life.

## Unbalancing Others

Being able to unbalance and throw others is not the aim of the practice. It is a fun game, but so what? It's easy for the desire to dominate and control others to reenter the practice. That is why the practice is to yield. It is to connect with and to protect our balance. When we discover that we balance, we also discover that our balance naturally seeks to maintain itself. We learn that it is not by rooting in one place that our balance is maintained. It is maintained by allowing natural movement. As soon as we focus on a result, like getting our partner, we have replaced our natural function with some man-made mental function – some egoist function – namely winning.

So yes, it is fun to play with our balance and the balance of others, but not for the sake of winning. Not for the sake of domination and control. Part of this is the desire for acknowledgment, for recognition from outside of ourselves. Look how skilled I am. Look how great I am. We attempt to fill up the hole where we are not acknowledging and appreciating ourselves. What we really seek is to know our true nature, to know our oneness and wholeness. To experience no separation and no collision is oneness. This is fullness. When we know this – who we are – nothing else matters. We don't need to achieve anything. We need no recognition. Rather than domination, we seek to join. How can we harmonize with others if we cannot harmonize with the earth and sky?

It is important to remember that our practice is not about increasing skills. In the end, as our bodies age and get sick, we lose our skill and our strength. We lose everything we have worked so hard to build up. What we are talking about in *fang sung* is not waiting until the end to lose everything. You can let go of it now. Just let it all drop. All of our projects. All of our attempt to make ourselves better. How about discovering who or what we actually are right now? What is the nature of being human? What is the nature of standing on the earth? The answers to these questions are not mental. They are bodily felt sensations. We are experiencing the nature of being human right now. We don't need to improve ourselves. We only need to uncover what is already here but has been covered up, a masterpiece that has been covered with paint and painted over. When we remove the paint, we see there is a masterpiece underneath. The thing is, we never take the time to uncover the paint. In fact we are busy adding more and more. *Fang sung* is to stop adding paint, stop trying to improve ourselves and instead just be present.

Unbalancing others is just a game. In fact, we do not seek to unbalance others. We seek to restore balance. Balance seeks balance. The nature of balance is to change. There are many ways to make numbers add up to 10, yet they all equal 10. Balance is not maintaining 1+9. Balance is maintaining 10. It is because life seeks to maintain balance that when 9 changes to 8, 1 changes to 2. Always 10. Always wholeness. The change is natural. It is about staying connected, not about domination. It is not one up and one down. It is up and down and up and down and all around. We don't seek to maintain a position or posture. We allow ourselves to change as the things around us change. We don't need to make change happen. It is already happening. We can resist it or not; however, the change still occurs because it is the nature of life. We seek to know the nature of life, and we know it by knowing our bodies. Our bodies are a microcosm of the macrocosm. We allow the change. We don't fight or resist it. We simply let go.

## Prison

All systems are prisons. This is what my *sifu* shared with me. They are prisons because they do not allow for our natural expression. Aikido is a system. Therefore aikido is a prison. Why is it a prison? In aikido we are told that certain responses are right or wrong. Do this and don't do that. I have only two guidelines. Don't fall down, and don't use extra effort. How do I respond to energy? What is an attack? What I call an attack is simply an attempt to upset my balance. It is a change in the environment that affects my balance. My system has a response to this. It is to seek balance. Don't tell me that when my balance is upset I can only respond in certain ways. No, the system knows what it needs to do to restore balance. The question is whether I will allow the system to work. It is not conscious. I don't tell myself what to do to regain balance when I slip on a banana peel. My body knows what it needs to do to regain balance. Why, when my balance is affected by another, do I need to learn techniques for regaining balance?

Standing up and not falling down is our natural ability. The art is about cultivating this natural ability, not about learning pre-programmed routines. The ability to stand up and not to fall down is natural. Standing on two feet is the highest evolution of human beings. What is the felt sense of balance? Balance is an experience. It is here and now. We stand in order to experience the bodily felt sense of balance. Autonomy is standing on one's own two feet. This is our freedom, our relationship with heaven and earth. What is it to stand between heaven and earth? It is to balance. The environment changes. Can we change with the changes, or are we attached to our position? Balance – the experience of not falling down – depends not on standing in one position. It is the capacity to allow ourselves to be moved, to be touched, not to resist the changes but to allow them in our own bodies. There is nothing to defend. My balance does not need to be defended.

Aikido, or any other system, says I need to respond in $y$ way to $x$ change. Why am I allowing my mind to decide this? $X$ and $y$ are two poles of one system. The key is in harmonization, becoming one. If I am one, then when $x$ changes, $y$ also will change. So the art is in harmonization. *Aiki*. Intent. Aikido is the study of intent. Is my intent to dominate and control, or is my intent to harmonize? We are already one being. Recognize the connection that already exists.

# NONRESISTANCE

*Aikido is the principle [of] non-resistance. Because it is non-resistant, it is victorious from the beginning. Those with evil intentions or contentious thoughts are instantly vanquished. Aikido is invincible because it contends with nothing.*

*- Morehei Ueshiba*

## Nonresistance

The important thing is to yield, to face fire with water, to be able to yield and follow. Nonresistance is a means of maintaining my equilibrium. Not fighting against anything. Not resisting anything. Allowing it for the sake of maintaining my center. Not sacrificing what I care about. Not having to defend myself. Not having to dominate or control others. Letting life be. Allowing myself to move in whatever way is necessary to maintain my equilibrium, to maintain my vertical line – my connection to heaven and earth. This is what is most important. Not giving up my birthright. I don't need to do anything to anyone, I simply maintain my relationship with heaven and earth. This is my primary relationship and this comes first. My body naturally does whatever it needs to do to maintain my relationship with heaven and earth. This is why we stand – to bring awareness to the body's relationship to earth and heaven. Let's start with earth. To allow myself to *fang sung.* To let go into the earth. To allow myself to be held and supported by the earth. To receive the abundance and the bounty of the earth. To feel my feet where they touch the earth. To feel my mass making contact with the mass of the earth. To feel that attraction. My body wants to return to the earth. I allow it to. I no longer brace against the earth. I breathe in, I tense and charge, I exhale and release and let go into the earth. I breathe in the energy of the earth through my feet, up my spine, to the top of my head, out the top of my head. I exhale and allow it to flow all around me and back down to the earth. This is not an exercise. This is paying attention to what is. We don't need to create anything extra. We are inquiring into the nature of being embodied. What are the sensations? What am I aware of?

So often we are busy making something without understanding what is present. When the colonists came to America, they built on top of a thriving civilization connected to nature. They did not pay attention. They did not see. They were so busy wanting to conquer, to dominate, that they failed to see what was already here. It's like that. A miraculous system is already here that keeps us alive. What is the nature of this system and what can it do? What is the potential here? That is what we are exploring: the system that steadies us when we slip on a banana peel. Or the system that heals our wounds naturally. We don't need to intervene. The system functions. Nature functions. Life functions. Life works easily and naturally. We don't need to interfere. Noninterference. First, do no harm. Don't get in the way of what is already working. Mind is not required. Mindfulness is – simply witnessing, paying attention. I am not the doer of the deed. I am simply the witness. This is the quality I want to bring into my practice. I allow my body to respond naturally, easily and effortlessly. I witness. I say yes. It is all part of a larger movement I may not be aware of. There is change. I allow the change. I do not resist. I allow. I feel the change. I allow myself to change with the larger change.

## Know Yourself

Transformation is not a process of addition. It is not a process of getting better or adding more skill. We are not looking to attain anything. In fact, quite the contrary. We are looking to let go of everything we have learned that is no longer necessary. We seek to experience the nature of energy just as it is prelinguistically, pre-culturally. We seek to experience the body directly, to experience the flow of life force energy directly – not mediated by anything or anyone. To know ourselves. We don't need to add anything. We seek to know our own nature as whole and complete. Not whole and complete as a separate entity, but whole and complete because I am part of all that is. That I have direct access to my self. Not mediated through anyone or anything. It is not learned. It is not achieved or attained. It is here now. It is what I am. I seek to know myself. To know my capacity. To know myself as possibility. Not as a thing but as an opening, a space of possibility. That is what I am cultivating. I am cultivating my self as a space of possibility, an opening for action. I do not know who or what I am. I know what I have been told, what we all have been told about who or what we are. We are born, grow old and die. We don't believe anything we have been told. We need to find out for ourselves. What is true for us? We need to trust our own experience, our own innate knowing.

When we practice, we are exploring who or what we are. We are getting to know ourselves. We are getting to experience ourselves, our connection to all that is. We are experiencing ourselves experiencing ourselves. It is about allowing everything to be just the way it is. Nonresistance, noninterference with what is. I don't need to change anything. How would I change it? What would I do? What needs to stay and what needs to go? My mind does not know the answers to these questions. I cannot figure it out and fix it. I can only let go. I can only non-resist. I can only allow. I can feel. I can experience. I can let it all be just the way it is without thinking I need to fix it or change it or make it better. I simply need to let go. This then, is the practice. Letting go. *Fang Sung.*

## Releasing Domination and Control

Rather than trying to dominate and control, we ask ourselves what we are afraid of. We are afraid of being dominated and controlled by others. We believe we live in a world in which we are dominated and controlled or we dominate and control others. This is what we have been taught. There are winners and there are losers. There is always one up and one down. We are calling into question this way of seeing the world. Who are we defending? We are defending an identity that does not exist. This whole game is based on the assumption that we are all separate and that there is not enough for everyone. It is based on separation and scarcity. This is not true. This is what we have been taught. We are interested in seeing the truth. The truth is we are all one. We are all aspects of the divine. All parts of nature. There is no separation. Separation is made in the mind. God created one world. God extends himself/herself. When we are defending, we are defending a false sense of self. We are defending this belief in separation and scarcity.

We desire to know another world, a world of kindness, of abundance, of purity, of wholeness and health. The world the God/Goddess created. Our birthright. To know this world, we must question everything we have been told. We must learn to think for ourselves. We must open to gnosis, to our own inner wisdom. We have been taught we don't know anything, that all knowledge exists outside of ourselves. Gnosis is our own innate knowing, our intuition. Don't believe anything I say to you. Find out for yourself what is true. Discover it for yourself. What is the world you want to live in? Separation and scarcity, or oneness and abundance? What are we looking for? What actions are we trying to justify? My actions of defense, of control and manipulation are justified by my belief that it is an us-versus-them world. In an us-versus-them world, my actions appear righteous. We need to question this belief in separation and scarcity.

Nonresistance means there is nothing, no physical position, to defend. I am able to move. You want this spot of ground, you may have it. I am not attached to any one position. My balance, my equilibrium, does not depend on my rootedness. My balance is a moving, dynamic balance. Being static is not the same as being balanced. In fact, my unwillingness to change with the changes is what unbalances me. I am holding on to a particular position, a particular point of view. This holding on makes me rigid and easily unbalanced. I don't need to defend myself. There is nothing to defend. I have no position. I have no one point of view. I am in motion, constantly changing in relation to my environment. I coevolve with my environment. I surrender to this coevolving process. I don't need to know where it is going. I am not coevolving to produce any result. I am coevolving for the experience of coevolution. I am surrendering and letting go of what I think needs to happen. I am allowing whatever needs to happen to happen and I trust that I will evolve with that, that I will change and transform with that. I am not trying to hold on to anything. I am allowing myself to be touched, to be changed, to be transformed. We move from trying to dominate and control to coevolving together, to changing and transforming together. It is a change of intent.

## Nonresistance to What Is

I seek the freedom to respond authentically in each moment, to maintain my equilibrium. There is no set way that I want to move or to interact or respond. There is no right way. The only right way is not to fall down and not to use excess effort. Every response will be different because every situation is different. What is not different is the feeling of nonresistance. I have no form and no intent. I am simply present with what is and allow myself to respond appropriately – naturally. It is not contrived.

The problem I have with aikido is that it is a system and therefore a prison. There are set ways of responding to the situation – *ikyo*, *nikyo*, *sankyo* and so forth. What if we can engage wholeheartedly and allow whatever forms that manifest to manifest? It's really about where I am coming from in my heart. Do I seek to dominate and control, or do I seek to understand? Do I seek to understand your point of view and where you are coming from? Can I allow your point of view? Can I allow your perspective? Does it need to be win/lose or is there another way of approaching the situation? Is there a way for both of us to be empowered through our interaction?

Do I recognize our oneness, or do I see us as separate beings with separate interests? Is there enough for all of us? It is not about learning skills so I can dominate and control you – so I can get my way. The opportunity is to see the situation in a new way in which we are not separate – we are one. It is the intent of oneness, of joining, of forgiveness. I am not against you. I do not stand against anything. I stand for love, for kindness, for compassion, for healing, for transformation, for truth, for oneness. This is what I stand for. I am the space, the context in which it all occurs.

Its not about domination and control. In domination and control, I win by doing something to you. In true *aiki*, I am not interested in doing anything to you. I am interested in holding a space in which you can know yourself as life force energy and you can harmonize with this energy. The practice is an internal one. It's not about winning over others. It is about winning over the discord in your own mind and heart. It is about you coming into harmony with life. This is the way: an awareness of being in harmony, a bodily felt experience of being in harmony with all that is. We are in harmony with gravity. We stand up and don't fall down. Yet we take this experience for granted. In *zhan zhuang*, we turn our attention to the physical sensations of standing up and not falling down. We already are experiencing this – now we are turning our conscious awareness to this experience. We are feeling it fully. We are enjoying it. This is a beautiful experience. This is the opportunity. This is the practice.

## Finite versus Infinite Games

It means going from a finite game to an infinite game. A finite game has a beginning and an end. There are only two outcomes of a finite game – winning or losing. I play to win. That is the point of the game. In an infinite game, I play for the sake of playing. The aim is to continue to play. There are an infinite number of outcomes. I am playing in order to learn and for the joy of play. The outcome is irrelevant to me. What matters is play. If I must do it, then it is not an infinite game. I choose to play. The difference between finite and infinite games is the difference between training and education. I am not simply repeating the past. I am new. I am engaging in a process of discovery. I don't know what will be discovered. The future is open in an infinite game. In a finite game, I am looking to produce one particular outcome. That outcome is me winning and you losing. In an infinite game, I am not concerned with winning and losing. I don't even know what winning and losing looks like.

A finite game is me versus you. An infinite game is me and you. I am no longer in resistance to you. I am yielding. I am no longer trying to dominate and control. No separation and no collision. No resistance. Yet I also do not fall down. I do not give up my balance. No resistance and no giving up my balance. Hence, don't fall down and don't use extra strength. Learn to yield – to let go, to not resist, to not fight against. I think it is important to understand what kind of a game we are playing. Is aikido being played as a finite or an infinite game? That is the question.

Do I need to defeat you in order to feel good about myself? Do I need to overpower you, impose my will upon you, in order to feel good about myself? This is different from protecting myself. This is transforming the situation from me versus you to me and you. That is aikido. I do that by not resisting you, by not playing a finite game. Just because you are playing a finite game does not mean I need to play a finite game. I can play an infinite game no matter what game you are playing. It doesn't matter. I have no interest in playing a finite game.

# YIN AND YANG

*Taiji is born from Wuji. It is the mother of Yin and Yang.*
*In movement Taiji separates; in stillness Yin and Yang*
*reunite and return to Wuji.*

*- Wang Zongyue*

## Body As a Vehicle

We are interested in returning to the Way, realigning ourselves with
nature. We call this the "natural state." It is man in alignment with
nature, living in a way that recognizes the sacredness of all things. It
is recognizing that all of us – two-legged, four legged and winged – all
come from the same source. We are all part of one creation. We seek to
align with this source. We initiate this process by aligning physically
with nature. We align ourselves with what we call gravity. We align
with the earth. The fact is that when we simply stand, we discover
we are already in alignment. We stand up and don't fall down. We
become aware of our center of equilibrium. This is key. The somatic
awareness of our equilibrium. Our point of balance. We are balancing.
What allows us to balance? We rest in balance. It is not something
we need to do or achieve. We are like those toys that no matter how
often you try to knock them over, they always bounce right back, like

a homing mechanism always seeking home. That home is effortless balance, alignment with the force of gravity.

The illusion is that we are separate, that everything we see is simply an object – something to manipulate and control. This worldview arises out of fear. And this fear arises out of the illusion that I am this body. That I was born and will die when this body was born and dies. I confuse my identity with this physical form. It is not that I am not this physical form. However, that is not all I am. I am not just this physical body. This physical body is nature; it is part of nature. The body is a microcosm of the universe. It is made of yin and yang. Or, to be more accurate, it expresses yin and yang.

We are interested in knowing the truth, our appropriate and true place in this universe. We need to question everything. It is all just a story that we believe. Different cultures live in different stories, different narratives about who we are and why we are here. These narratives change over time. We are interested in the experience, not the story. The experience lives in our bodily felt sensations free of any stories. Each of us is in alignment. We stand up and don't fall down. We bring our awareness to our physical alignment. That which is present without any effort of our own. This is grace. This alignment is grace. We do not cause it. We did not create ourselves or this world. It is given to us freely. Our alignment is given. It is not made through our effort. It is through our willingness to discover it that we become aware. It is our desire to know ourselves as part of this creation that we discover our alignment with it.

The process is one of return. From the many we discover two – yin and yang. We discover that yin and yang are two poles of one process and that this process is life. Life is change, the movement from yin to yang. Emptiness and fullness are two aspects of breathing, two sides of the same coin. We seek to return to, to know, this natural state, this state of oneness with all that is. We use the body as a vehicle for discovering our natural state. The body is a vehicle for discovering our true relationship with nature and all that is. We start here with what is present – our physical body. By being present and exploring the nature of our physical bodies we discover the nature of the universe.

## From *Wuji* to *Taiji*

To be balanced is your nature. This is what my teacher said to me. This is what we discover when we stand. We discover being balanced is our nature. In other words, we don't need to make ourselves balance with our conscious minds. All our efforts, anything we seek to do, to achieve, to produce, does not add to our balance. We are already in perfect balance. It is our nature to balance. Balancing is our natural ability. Balancing means not falling down. It means being in harmony with the force of gravity. When we release partial tension in our bodies, we naturally stand up and don't fall down. Balancing requires no extra effort. In fact, any extra effort we use takes us out of balance.

We are, for the most part, unaware of our natural state. Our natural state is like water to fish. We just don't see it. We don't need to achieve it; we only need to pay attention. The exercise is an exercise in awareness. The balancing is already happening. We are doing it all the time. Or rather, it is happening all of the time without conscious intervention. We are simply directing our awareness there. We are paying attention to our natural ability. As we appreciate it, it grows. Not because we are doing anything to it. We can't pull the plant up to make it grow, but we can care for it – we can make sure it has good soil and plenty of sun and water. That is our job. We are simply becoming aware of our natural state.

We begin on two legs. *wuji* – a state of undifferentiation. *Wuji* leads to *taiji*. We can shift our equilibrium between our two legs. One is full and one is empty. Two poles. Tension and relaxation. Out of these two poles all techniques are born. In Taoism, we seek to reverse the process. From all of the techniques we find that they all contain yin and yang. We become aware of yin and yang in our movements. From there we trace it back to discover that in stillness it concentrates, it comes together as one – *wuji*. In movement it separates – *Taiji*. Movement and stillness are two poles of life. We discover our nature, our oneness with all that is. We discover that our bodies are a microcosm of the universe. In knowing ourselves, we know the world.

So the practice, as my teacher says, is not about developing skill. It is about knowing yourself. It is about knowing the natural state, who or what you are prior to language. Knowing the oneness of all that is. Knowing that there is no separation. Separation is of the mind. It only exists in our minds. In reality, all is one. This is a bodily felt experience. That is the point. The oneness is not just a concept or idea. We experience oneness, wholeness, in and through our bodies. We are scientists. We are discovering what is present. We return to experience. We are somatic phenomenologists. We are interested in what is actually present right here and right now in our bodies. We are interested in what is real, what is eternal. What was here before this body was born and what will remain when this body is gone. Not as an idea, but as a bodily felt experience. The bodily felt experience of what is. The wholeness of what is. All of it. Allowing it all to be. Non-resistance to what is. That is our practice.

## Distinguishing Yin and Yang

All living systems seek to preserve themselves. To the extent that human beings are living systems, we also seek to preserve ourselves. Preservation is different than control and manipulation. Preservation is not based on doing anything to anyone. It is really about boundaries. It is saying that I only agree to mutually beneficial relationships. It is standing for my right to safety and yours. It is not about me versus you. It is the recognition that we are all in this together. We will rise together or fall together. I am not trying to do anything to you. I am simply exercising my right to be free, to live in harmony with nature.

It is my life force that seeks to preserve itself. Mind is not involved. Living systems seek to preserve their equilibrium. Living systems change in order to continue to live and thrive. It is this capacity to change, to adapt, this resiliency, that we seek to cultivate. Physically speaking, it means we are not attached to one spot. My balance is not based on rooting in one spot. I am not a tree. I move. My balance is dynamic, not static. It is a moving balance. It is the movement from yin to yang to yin. Always in balance. One plus nine, two plus eight, three plus seven. They all equal ten. I don't need to control you to always give me one. You can give me force of two, three, seven, eight – it doesn't matter. I can adapt to meet your force to maintain ten. It is the ability to be tense or relaxed, empty or full. This is the training. I recognize yin and yang in my body. I bring awareness to that. The body will naturally provide the level of tension versus relaxation to preserve its own equilibrium. We must bring awareness to these two states of being. We must be able to distinguish yin and yang in the body.

We begin by standing in *wuji*, our original state. No differentiation between yin and yang. Not two. It is from this state of oneness in the body that we are able to identify yin and yang. In stillness our *qi* congeals. In movement it disperses. In stillness we know *wuji*. In movement we know *taiji*. From *taiji* all techniques are born. The techniques are a result of matching, of balancing my yin to your yang and my yang to your yin. The balancing process is a natural process. What prevents it is our attachment to particular movement patterns. Forget about the techniques and movement patterns. Come to understand yin and yang within your own body. This is the key. We cultivate the embodied distinction of yin and yang within our own bodies. We know it, not intellectually. We feel it, we experience it firsthand. Empty and full. Tense and relaxed. Two poles of one process. They are not separate – they are the extremes of one process. One movement.

## Pay Attention to the Movement

It is not about learning new movement patterns. Not about practicing movement patterns. No patterns, no habits. Each encounter is unique. This is not a repeat, not a copy. It is original movement sourced in the moment. Responding freely, naturally spontaneously to what is. Allowing what is and the natural response to it. These are one movement. Two hands moving together, staying connected. What matters is the connection. The quality of the connection. The responsiveness, the capacity to respond, to be touched, to be moved. Not mentally constructed movement. The tiger has no need to practice anything. He is a tiger and is being a tiger. He will defend himself when threatened. Just as we naturally seek to maintain our equilibrium. The system is designed to maintain equilibrium, just as our system, our body is also designed to maintain equilibrium. To not fall down, to balance. This is our natural function. What is true for the microcosm is true for the macrocosm. It is all one system.

We can experience the Tao within our own bodies. This is what we seek to allow. The Tao is always functioning. We simply get out of the way, allowing it and paying attention to it. This is the object of our meditation – the body's natural ability to balance. This is where we place our attention, on the movement – the mindless movement. The universal movement. We place our awareness on the rotation of the earth. Not out there, but inside of us. The universal life movement – the play of yin and yang within our own bodies for the sake of maintaining equilibrium. This is the object of our attention. Heavenly movement within our own body. This is the movement of god/goddess/allthatis. We did not cause this movement. This movement birthed us and it continues to move. It is moving now within and without. Pay attention to this movement within your own body.

## Aiki Body

What is an *aiki* body? It is a body that is harmonized with *qi*. My body is an expression of my intent. Is my intent to harmonize, to join, or is my intent to dominate and control? This is really what it comes down to. My intent to dominate and control is based on the illusory belief that this is a zero-sum game. There is not enough to go around. There is not enough for both you and me, so I will get mine. It based on lack, scarcity and fear. This lack, scarcity and fear is a call for love. A call for oneness. I attack because I am afraid. I am afraid because I misunderstand who I am. I am ignorant. I pray to have my eye open so that I can see and know the truth of oneness. The truth that I am not separate from you – that we are one body. We are connected. We are one. When I engage it is to bring peace and healing. It is to help everyone to follow their own path. My engagement is love. It is non-resistance. I am not trying to get anyone to do anything. I am simply moving in a way that allows me to maintain my own equilibrium. That is all. I am not trying to do anything to you other than to fully receive you, listen to you, allow all of you to be present. I can allow you to have your way, to go your way.

I will, however, protect my equilibrium. I can move out of harm's way. That is my practice. Maintaining my balance and equilibrium in all situations. Allowing myself to change with the changes. No position to protect. No land to protect. My balance is not based on a particular posture. The postures are always changing – what doesn't change is my equilibrium – my balance. This is what we are paying attention to – the bodily felt sense of balance. An *aiki* body is a balanced body. An *aiki* body moves effortlessly. It moves to maintain its own equilibrium without the direction of my mind. It naturally maintains equilibrium. This is its natural ability. This is what I seek to cultivate. I begin working with the force of gravity. I notice how my body yields in order to maintain its equilibrium in gravity. I then notice how this same intelligence is at play when I lift up my suitcase. My body naturally knows how it needs to adjust to maintain balance. This natural ability can be allowed to function when I engage with another. My body naturally adjusts to your attack to maintain its equilibrium. This is the function of the *aiki* body – to maintain equilibrium.

This is *taiji*: not *taijiquan* the exercise, but *taiji* the principle. The continuous play of yin and yang. 1+9=10, 2+8=10. When you give me 1, my body naturally responds with 9 in order to maintain balance. I don't need to think about this. I don't need to direct it with my mind. This is a function of the *aiki* body. The practice is a practice of awareness. As I appreciate this natural ability, it appreciates. I am simply drawing attention to it. Again, we don't become more effective at pulling our hand away from a hot stove by practicing moving our hand away. We become more effective by becoming more sensitive. We become more sensitive through awareness. Awareness of our natural ability and the bodily felt experience of balancing.

# YI

*The secret of internal work does not lie in movements, but
in the intention. This point is a key element in the transition
from Wai Gong (External Work) to Nei Gong (Internal
Work).*

*- Serge Augier*

## Desire

The starting point of *yiquan* is desire. It is what I long for in my heart.
I long for love, for wholeness, for union with earth and heaven. It is
this longing to know my true self that is the source of *yiquan*. This is
*yi*. Without this feeling, the art is empty. So we start with that longing
to return to *wuji*. Oneness. Not two. When we stand we connect with
our hearts and the desire in our hearts to return to the source of all.
We relax and release. Release all that is not ours, everything we have
been taught and told into the earth. We stop doing. We give up our
ideas of what needs to happen. We give up any goal. We become aware
that we are standing. We are balancing upon the earth. Yet we are not
thinking about balancing. It is just happening. The body is moving
ever so slightly in order to maintain balance. The body knows what to
do to maintain balance. There is a self-regulatory function. When I eat
food that is bad for me, I vomit it. When I am cut, the body naturally

heals the wound. When I stand up, I naturally balance. I don't need to think about it. I could not control all the minute movements with my mind that I need in order to balance. When I slip on a banana peel, my body will naturally attempt to regain balance. There is no set way of regaining balance. Not set movements. I cannot teach you the movements to regain balance when your balance is challenged.

Balancing is a natural ability. We all have this ability. This ability to come into balance. To maintain balance with the changes in our environment. Often we don't want to change. The world around us is constantly changing, but we want to stay the same. The nature of life is change and the unknown. We don't know where it is going or what it will look like. It is the art of changing with change. It is what we do. If I pick up a briefcase full of bricks, my body knows what it needs to do to maintain its balance. My body adjusts. It is this capacity to adjust. This capacity to change that we want to cultivate. The capacity to change is what allows us to find union. It is in the service of our *yi* – our desire for oneness and wholeness – that we cultivate our natural ability to adapt. What does it mean to adapt? It means I allow this process to happen. I allow myself to balance and I pay attention to it. It is always happening, but we are not aware of it. In standing, we bring our awareness to our natural ability of balancing. We get to know it. We become intimate with it. We are not a tree. We are not rooted in the ground, yet we are able to stand up and not fall down. What is it that allows this? More importantly, what is the bodily felt sense of standing up and not falling down? We are embodying the somatic distinction of balance.

So, if you attack me, if you attempt to effect my balance, my body naturally responds in a way that allows me to continue to stand up and not fall down. It's not about maintaining a position. It's about balancing in every position. It's about finding balance right where you are in this situation. Not changing you or the situation but allowing myself to change to maintain my equilibrium.

## Yi

We need to distinguish between heavenly movement and egoic movement. Egoic movement is controlled by the small mind. It is a copy. I am attempting to copy someone else's movement. True movement originates from within. It is not a copy. It is original movement that comes from within. It originates in stillness. As I allow the water to calm, the dirt sinks and I am left with clear water. I cannot experience or inquire into clear water until I am willing to allow the dirt to sink. As long as I am active, moving, the dirt cannot sink. When the dirt sinks, I am left with the experience of clear water. I begin to notice the water. I notice that there are currents and eddies in the water, not caused by me. There is a flow. I don't make this flow. It is of the nature of water to flow.

The art is about discovering this movement. That is the beginning. There is something happening here. The tree is growing. I don't see it grow each day, but after a year it is substantially bigger than it was. It is a different tree. This is the nature of life – change. I don't need to make it happen. I can support it. I can make sure that the tree isn't peed on by dogs. I can make sure it has enough water and sunshine. But the growing just happens. I don't need to set a goal. Also, the tree itself is not less valuable when it is small than when it is large. It is not like the tree is saying to itself: "If only I can be a tree that gives fruit, then I would be a real tree." It is a real tree now. It is engaged in a process.

Our art is an expression of our intent. Is the intent to dominate and control or is the intent to find harmony? It starts in the heart. It is a manifestation of what is in my heart. A desire for oneness and harmony, or a desire for domination and control. Which one is it? Domination and control arise out of my fear of being dominated and controlled. It is a triangle. Only one person can be on top. What I am talking about is a circle. We are all one. We are all in the same boat. We will rise or fall together.

I don't want to practice someone else's art. I want to practice my art. It doesn't need to look a certain way. What matters is the *yi*. What matters is what is in my heart. All proceeds from this. It's not about subduing others. Let me pay attention to the fear in my own heart. The fear of being dominated and controlled. It is about standing up for myself and defending my right to live, to thrive. Standing for life. Standing for trust. Standing for truth. Standing for freedom and equality. This is what I stand for. Not about doing anything to anyone. Being in harmony with all that is. Standing up, not falling down is being in harmony with the force of gravity. Let me begin with that. Paying attention to where I am in harmony through no effort of my own. I am created in harmony. I am part of this glorious creation. I have a place, a natural place in harmony with all that is. I don't need to figure it out. I simply pay attention to not falling down. Pay attention to my body in space in harmony with heaven and earth. That is all. Simply noticing. Simply paying attention to what already is.

## Heavenly *Yi*

I don't want to get into a conflict. Yet I will not let myself be abused. I will protect and nourish my life energy. This is natural and this is my right. I have a right to be and to express myself. I have a right to my own thoughts and feelings. I validate myself. I don't need approval from others, acceptance from others, anything from others to feel good about myself. I am not looking to achieve anything. I am simply wanting to be in harmony with life. To be one. Or rather, to know my oneness with all that is. That is my intent. It is important to keep this in mind. I don't need to be better than others, nor am I worse than others. We all have the same worth and value, not because of what we have done, but because of who we are. Because we are part of life. All things are temporary. Not the source. The source is love. Extending love naturally because that is what love does. Love extends. Love includes. Love honors and respects. That is the nature of love and that is the source of who I am.

So, yes, I want to learn. I want to learn who or what I am. I want to learn how to coordinate with others in equality. The winners and losers. Nonhierarchical. No up and down. I want to learn how to harmonize with the life energy that flows in and through me. I want to let go, release and surrender to the earth. I don't want to fight, yet I will stand for what I care about. I will stand up for myself and not allow myself to be abused in any way.

I don't need to depend on my own strength. My own strength is nothing. It is about aligning my intent with the intent of the universe. That intent is to extend love. It is an expression of love. I don't need to depend on my strength. I am not going to produce the result that is needed here on my own. There is an intent. An intent of wholeness, of oneness of coming home to love. That is the intent of the universe. To shine. I can surrender and let go into this intent.

## We Are All Already Centering

What is the center? The center is the still place within our bodies around which all else revolves. It is that which we seek to conserve. It is our connection to the earth. Center is not a location. It is an experience. Everything has a center. It is this connection to the earth that we seek to conserve. Unless we maintain this connection we will not survive as a species. We are part of the Gaian system. This being part of Gaia is a bodily felt experience. We are magnetically drawn to the earth. We stand on two legs and we don't fall down. This standing up is no longer a conscious effort on our part. Yes, we learned to stand and balance as children, but now we no longer think about it – we take it for granted. We take this centering – this balancing process for granted. I am going to call this balancing process *taiji*: the Great Ultimate. The poles are yin and yang. There is a relationship between yin and yang. They are not separate. They are two poles of one process. The process we call centering. We are doing it all of the time in order to stand up and not fall down. We don't need to learn to center – we are already doing it. If we didn't know how to do it, we would not be standing up. All we are doing is directing our attention to this natural ability. We are experts at centering. We have been doing it for most of our lives. We just have not been aware of it. We have been blind to it. Now, we are simply becoming aware of what we already effortlessly do. In appreciating our natural ability, it naturally appreciates. It grows, it becomes stronger through our paying attention to it.

I cannot teach you how to center. Centering is fundamental to being a bipedal primate. We do it naturally. The question now is are we willing to feel it. Are we willing to become intimate with this process? To see how it works. To notice that when we slip on the ice our body does whatever it needs to do to maintain its equilibrium. This is true of the earth. This is true of Gaia. The system is designed to be self-regulating. To maintain equilibrium. This is the gift, the miracle each of us has been given by being born into a human body. We simply allow this centering process, this balancing process to work. We allow it. That is the practice – letting go and allowing. Paying attention. Feeling. Can I teach you the movement your body needs to make in order to balance? Of course not. Each situation is unique and your body already knows what it needs to do to maintain balance. It is already doing it.

It's not about learning how to center. You already know how to. In fact, you are an expert at centering. You just don't recognize it. You don't pay attention to it. When we practice *zhan zhuang*, we are paying attention to this natural ability. We are feeling it work. This process is ecstatic. It is the working of God/Goddess within us. It is *taiji*. The interplay of substantial and insubstantial for the sake of standing up and not falling down. For the sake of harmonizing with the force of life. What matters here is intent. The intent is to join in love. To recognize our oneness with all that is. The intent is not to dominate and control. It is to allow. This is the process. Allowing our natural ability to center. We seek to cultivate our natural ability and we do this with our *shen*. With our awareness. We pay attention to it. We experience it. We feel the bodily felt sensation of centering. We are doing it all of the time. We are just choosing to become aware of *taiji* within our own bodies. We discover it in stillness. It arises in stillness and leads us into movement. The *yi* guides *qi*.

## Knowing Myself

Harmonizing with life energy begins with my own life energy. It begins with becoming aware of my own *qi*, *ki* or life energy. I feel it bodily. I become aware of the life force energy flowing in and through me. This is where it begins. Life force energy allows me to stand up and not fall down. No life force energy – no standing, no balancing. The nature of *qi* is to balance. Yin and yang. Stillness and motion. What is the nature of life force energy? This is what I seek to know. It is in me. I simply turn my attention to it. I turn my attention away from the external world. I stop doing. I stop the world. I do this by turning my attention within. I am not seeking to learn anything, to change anything, to improve myself in any way. I am simply interested in knowing what I am. Knowing the life force energy as it manifests as me. I feel it. It is a bodily felt sensation and I turn my attention to it.

What I conserve is an intention. An intention that shows up in me and in you. Heavenly *yi*. The desire for joining and oneness. The desire for true *aiki*. For true harmony. For oneness. For self-realization. This is what I conserve. I don't need to do anything. All is given. I am as God created me. Not separate. I am part of something much bigger than I think I am. I am part of life. This energy, this force animates all things. Brings life to all things. What is this? I seek to know this energy. Aikido is the path or way of harmonizing with *qi*. It is not something we do. It is something we are. It is recognizing that we are in harmony with all that is. We are in harmony with all that is, because we are a part of all that is. We don't need to make harmony. Harmony already exists. We choose to become aware of it or not.

Not domination, not power, but love. Love of all that is. This is what I conserve. I am not seeking to be better than anyone. I am seeking to join, to know that I am one with all that is. That is my intent. The movements, the techniques (if there are such things) arise out of this. *Yi* is my desire, it is what is in my heart. This desire for oneness, for joining, for love. This is what guides me. I don't need to learn how to respond. Response naturally arises from perception. The question is: "What is the world I perceive?" Is it a world of separation or of oneness? What do I choose to see? Do I choose to see the God/Goddess in you? Do I look upon the world in forgiveness or with grievances? How do I choose to harmonize with my world? What does it mean to live in harmony with heaven and earth?

It is a process of awareness. A process of letting go and surrendering to what is. A process of allowing. We are not seeking to add one iota to our height. We cannot do it even if we want to. It's about seeing what is. What is true. I balance. I stand up and don't fall down. I don't do this. This is my natural ability. I seek to know this, to cultivate this natural ability of remaining in balance with all that is. I don't do it. I am in balance, naturally. I take the time to experience this fully. To know myself as being in balance with all that is. To know myself as balancing. I balance – naturally with no effort at all. No effort is necessary. It balances. This is its nature.

## Zhan

In stillness
Stand upon the Earth
Cultivate feeling awareness
Of not falling down
Body naturally manifests
Movement before mind
Effortless engagement
Balances all forces